CHANGE YOUR
PARADIGM,
CHANGE
YOUR LIFE

CHANGE YOUR PARADIGM, CHANGE YOUR LIFE

Flip That Switch NOW!

BOB PROCTOR

FOREWORD BY SANDY GALLAGHER

Published 2021 by Gildan Media LLC
aka G&D Media
www.GandDmedia.com

Front Cover design by Patti Knoles

Interior design by Meghan Day Healey of Story Horse, LLC

Library of Congress Cataloging-in-Publication Data is available upon request

ISBN: 978-1-7225-0561-5

10   9   8   7   6   5   4   3   2   1

Contents

Foreword
by Sandy Gallagher

*H*ave you ever wondered why hard work is often not enough to produce the results you've been hoping for in your career? Have you been puzzled about why, despite years of setting goals, you continue to fall short of your targets year after year? Are you curious why, when stressful circumstances happen in society or in your personal life, you find it difficult to control your attitude and emotions while others seem to stay calm, collected, and confident? Traditional personal development advice, such as thinking positively, visualizing what you want, or affirmations, too often feels like rolling a boulder uphill rather than the effortless, exciting, downhill process that you were expecting.

The answer to these common personal development questions lies in a factor that few success or motivational speakers, teachers, or philosophers ever address. This factor, which completely controls your long-term success or failure, is your paradigm.

In this book, motivational legend and personal development expert, Bob Proctor will present some incredible material that was previous only available to his attendees of his exclusive, sold-out seminars. Here you will get a master's level education and learn how to get results in a systematic, consistent, and sustainable way, bypassing the worst effects of success killers like fear of failure, fear of success, procrastination, and the very worst: self-sabotage.

Bob will show you how to handle it all by spending time working on your paradigm—the one thing that the vast majority of people overlook, but the one that's the most important.

Just what is a paradigm? As Bob will teach you, at its most basic level, a paradigm is a mental program situated in your subconscious that has almost exclusive control over all your habitual behavior—and almost all of your behavior is habitual.

Paradigms are a multitude of habits passed down from generation to generation, and they manifest themselves in many ways. Paradigms are the way you view yourself, the world, and opportunity. They are how you approach change and challenges. Once you realize that all of your behavior is controlled by paradigms, the way you look at the entire world will change.

Perhaps you know someone who seems habitually angry, upset at every turn in life, and unable to see the positive in any situation. Maybe you know someone who has battled fluctuating weight for years or decades. They seem to be on track for a while, getting healthy and dropping pounds, but they always seem to bounce back to where they once were. Perhaps you know someone who seems to be stuck at a certain level of income for years and can never seem to break through to the next level. All of these outcomes are controlled by paradigms. Just as paradigms can be a prison of one's making, they can also be changed to deliver you the freedom to be exactly the person you want to be.

In this book, Bob will give you the key to freeing yourself from limiting paradigms and to changing your paradigm—that underlying mental programming—to transform your finances, health, career, relationships, and life.

Bob Proctor is the perfect teacher to take you on this journey. Bob has studied the mind and human potential with some of the greatest minds the world has ever known. In 1961, he started studying the all-time success classic *Think and Grow Rich* by Napoleon Hill, and it transformed his life. Bob has listened to recordings by personal development legend Earl Nightingale thousands of times. Bob also worked shoulder to shoulder with Earl Nightingale and his company, the Nightingale-Conant

Corporation, from 1968 to 1973, before leaving to start his own personal development company, Proctor Gallagher Institute, with his partner and co-founder, Sandy Gallagher. Today millions have been inspired by Bob through the hit movie *The Secret*, his books, including his *New York Times* best seller *You Were Born Rich*, his coaching programs, and live events.

Chapter One

Your Awesome Power to Change

This is going to be an incredible book for some of you.

Why didn't I say, "*all* of you?" Because I want to stress the vital importance of making a decision to change your life. *You* decide if it's going to be you.

Changing your paradigm takes a committed decision, because it goes in the opposite direction of nearly everything we've been taught. We go to school, take a book, read it, ask questions on the material, and then go on to another book. The truth is, we can't possibly understand the contents of the book this way. Reading something once and moving on is not going to do it.

Our paradigm was built through repetition—constant, spaced repetition—and that's the way it's going to be changed. But this makes little sense to most people: they're relating to the way they have been and the way they were educated in the past, when they weren't really being educated at all; they were merely gathering information.

You'll see people with very impressive degrees from prestigious universities who are struggling through their life. They don't have enough money; they don't hold down a good position. If they have their own company, they go bankrupt or go out of business. You think, "They're so smart; how could this possibly happen?"

The truth is, they're not very smart at all. They've gathered a lot of information, but they don't use it. Their behavior is controlled by their paradigms, not by the information they've got. They're not doing what they know how to do. For some strange reason, they never figure it out. They never stop and analyze their own behavior in relation to what they know.

Over the years, I have found that most people who are highly successful have unconscious competence. They cannot articulate why they're doing so well. They may be multimillionaires and they may have built prestigious organizations, but they cannot transfer this knowledge to their children, because they don't know why they're doing it. They'll say, "Well, I just do it." People think these individuals are pretty smart, but it's got nothing to do with being smart. It has to do with their paradigm, because the paradigm controls us to an enormous degree.

Success in any undertaking totally depends on what's going on inside of our minds; it's got nothing to do with what's going on outside. Some people do extremely well even in the face of bad economic conditions. Even during the Great Depression, not everyone was out of work; not everyone was broke. Some people did very well, earning millions of dollars.

Why did they do very well? What was going on? Why did a few people win? They built their success in their minds. It has to come from the inside out, not from the outside in. We're being controlled by our outside world because we've been trained that way; we've been programmed to let the outside world control us.

Paradigms and Habits

As I've said, just thinking positively isn't going to do it; that's an illusion. It takes a change in paradigm, and a paradigm is a multitude of ideas that are fixed in our subconscious minds. Ideas that are fixed in our subconscious mind are known as *habits*. A paradigm is a multitude of habits that are fixed in our subconscious mind. A habit is an idea that expresses itself without any conscious thought; you just automatically move. You drive your car primarily by habit. You don't have to think to do it, because you've been programmed.

If you objectively observe your own behavior for two or three hours from the time you get up in the morning, you'll see that most of your behavioral patterns are not going to give you the success you desire. Then you have to ask yourself, "Why am I acting this way?"

Every day, you do the same things, because you're programmed to do them. We're programmed to live the way we're living. First of all, we're programmed genetically; that's why we look like our relatives; it's built right into our genes at birth. Each of us is the confluence of a genetic pool that goes back for many generations. It controls us; it controls everything we're doing. A person's paradigm has nothing to do with what they learned in school. If a person has a bad paradigm, they're going to lose, even if they have a great education. Their education is not going to help them.

First of all, we have to understand how the paradigm is formed. Then we have to understand how it's changed, and that is something most people do not understand. It's not taught in school. There are very few seminars that teach it. When I came across this idea, I was shocked, because even though I was working in this field, I didn't really understand this principle.

Unconscious Competence

Way back in 1961, I was earning $4,000 a year, I owed $6,000, and I couldn't see how I was ever going to get out of it. Five years later, I was earning over a million dollars a year, and I owned a company with branches in Toronto, Montreal, Boston, Cleveland, Atlanta, and London.

I was being very irresponsible. I was living in London; I had moved over there and started a company. I'd go to the Playboy Club and play roulette. I didn't care if I lost the money, because I knew where the money was and how to get it.

One day I stopped and asked, "How did this happen? Why did my life change so dramatically?" I couldn't answer this question. I didn't know why. I had been raised to believe that if you're going to earn a lot of money, you've got to be really smart. I knew I wasn't very smart, but I was earning a lot of money. Then I'd also been raised to believe that if you don't go to school, you'll never get a good job. I hadn't done this; I went to high school for two months. I didn't have a good job; I owned the whole company.

That's when I started to check almost everything I was raised to believe, and I found that most of it wasn't true. Can one person be better than someone else? No. No one is any better than anybody else. Their results may be a little better, they may earn more, they may be more productive, they may be able to run faster, but we're all exactly the same. If you took us all and put us into a fire, we're all going to be reduced to the same level. We're mass, energy, and vibration—color, size, gender don't mean anything. We are all the same. We've got to realize we are all subject to laws that are exact; they don't change. They weren't made by men, so men are not going to change them. Our success is going to depend on our understanding and our ability to bring our lives into harmony with these laws.

One day I had a euphoric experience, and everything in my head started to shift. I didn't know why I was acting as I was. I didn't know why I was winning. I had no formal education, no business experience. I thought, "I'm going to figure this out. I'm going to find out why I became successful."

It took me nine and a half years of conscious and deliberate focus to figure out the answer. When I did, all I wanted to do was work at it. I was in building maintenance; I'd started cleaning one office, and I ended up cleaning a lot of offices in a number of different cities. I left that and went to work at the Nightingale-Conant Corporation. I went from earning over $1 million a year to $18,000 a year. Five years later, I was earning $33,000.

I was prepared to pay them to let me work there because of the material they had. I thought Earl Nightingale and Lloyd Conant were absolute geniuses; what they were doing blew my mind. I didn't know anybody else that was doing what they were doing. I wanted to learn, and I did. I studied them like a scientist. That's when I started to connect the dots.

I was born during the Depression, and when I was only six years old, the whole world went to war; everything was rationed. I lived through some interesting times, when there was nothing but bad news. Nobody was interested in developing a child's mind. My mother was raising three, so getting by was the main deal.

In 1961, I started listening to Earl Nightingale's recordings on my little battery-operated record player, and I couldn't stop. I had never heard anybody talk like Earl Nightingale. I used to think that if God had a voice, it would be like his. Since then, I've become locked into this material; I've never stopped studying it from 1961 till today.

Developing Awareness

This material should be taught in schools, and even before that. You can actually teach it to a baby. We have, as a people, become obsessed with the development of the intellect, and we ignore the development of awareness. A person can have doctorates in two or three subjects and yet be unaware of how to earn money, how to build a business, or how to develop personally.

Awareness is the key. We want to become aware, I believe, of our oneness with God, with infinite intelligence. The more aware we become, the more it's reflected in our results. A lack of awareness is also reflected in our results.

One of Earl's most famous programs was *The Strangest Secret*, in which he said that you become what you think about. The more you look into that idea, the more profound it becomes. I've taken this a bit further by adding that we put the brakes on ourselves through how we choose our thoughts.

We have to start by understanding that there's only one part of the universe that we can change, and that is ourselves. We can change nothing else. We can't change the conditions or circumstances around us. We have to adapt to what's going on and keep going, but we also have to understand that we're bigger than the external situations that we're facing. I really don't give those things a lot of time, because they pass, and something else will come. There's always something outside that will control us if we let it. I don't choose to let it. I'm in control of me.

Furthermore, it's not just what we think; it's what we internalize, because you can think something without internalizing it. You've got to internalize these thoughts, you've got to emotionalize them, or they're not going to do you any good. If you keep them on a conscious level alone, you can be thinking of wealth and live in poverty. If you haven't internalized the thoughts of wealth, you're going to stay in poverty.

Neville Goddard, the inspirational author and speaker (who usually went by just "Neville"), put it very well: he said the future must become the present in the imagination of the one who has wisely and consciously created circumstances. We've been given mental faculties that no other form of life has been given; all the other little creatures in the world are completely at home in their environment; they blend in. We're totally disoriented because we've been given the mental faculties to create our environment, yet you can go right through our educational system and learn nothing about these higher faculties.

Memory, perception, will, reason, imagination, intuition—these are phenomenal powers, but do we understand how they work? As the late best-selling author Wayne Dyer said, "When you change the way you look at something, what you look at changes." If you change your perception, you change your world. We've got perfect memory; we've got perfect intuition; all of our higher faculties are perfect. They need developing, but we're not even taught we have them, so we're not taught how to use them. The imagination is not just something to play with. Everything we see, the world around us, was first created in the imagination and then turned into physical results. The world operates by law.

Aerospace engineer Wernher von Braun put it very well. When John Kennedy asked him, "What would it take to build a rocket that would carry a person to the moon and then bring him back safely to earth?" von Braun answered, "The will to do it."

The will is one of our higher faculties. It enables us to hold one idea on the screen of our mind to the exclusion of all outside distractions. When you focus on one idea, that idea must move into form. As Andrew Carnegie observed, any idea that's held in the mind, that's emphasized, that's either feared or revered, will begin at once to clothe itself in the most convenient and appropriate form available. One of the first laws of the universe is the perpetual transmutation of energy: energies are forever moving into form, through form, and back out of form.

Energy and Form

On a clear day, you can look up into the sky and see a little cloud gather. There's energy moving into form. Then the cloud will start to get dark and heavy, and boom! Out comes the water. If you stood there long enough, you would see the water go right back to where it came from. Energy returns to its source of origin: that's true with us and with everything that we use.

We're living with laws. Most people don't understand the laws, so they're not living in harmony most of the time. As we understand the laws and bring our life into harmony with them, things start moving in the right direction.

Ralph Waldo Emerson said the law of cause and effect is the law of laws: what you put out comes back.

If you give a lot of good, you're going to receive a lot of good, because you're putting yourself in harmony with it.

When *The Secret* come out, it did a lot of good, but it also confused many people. They believe in the law of attraction: think of it, and you will attract it. But most of the people that talk about law of attraction don't really understand it. The law of attraction is a secondary law. The primary law is the law of vibration. It decrees that everything moves; nothing rests. We live in an ocean of emotion, and we think on a frequency. Thought is energy.

The frequency you're thinking on is going to dictate what you attract to you, because it's going to control the vibration that you're in. You can't attract something that you're not in harmony with. If a person is poor, they have no money, they've never had any money, and they're thinking they're going to get rich, all they'll ever do is remain in poverty. They're in a poverty vibration. When they understand that and change it, they're in a different world, and they're playing a different game.

We believe that education is putting information in our heads, but that's not it at all. Maria Montessori, the famous educator, said, "We send children to school, and we think they're cups; we want them to fill up the cup. The truth is, the cups are already full." All the knowledge, all the power, there ever was or ever will be is omnipresent. You've already got all the knowledge and power you'll ever need. You don't get energy, you release it, and you release it to desire. When you've got a desire, you've got the energy to do it.

Our spiritual DNA is perfect. There's perfection within every one of us, and that perfection seeks to express itself within and through us. Spirit is always for expansion, for expression; it always show the essence of who we are as pure and unadulterated spirit. It always wants to express itself in a greater way. That's why we want things. Actually, we don't want to get, we want to grow: "I want to run faster; I want to jump higher." Spirit wants to express itself through us. We're spiritual beings. You'll hear people say they're having a spiritual experience. They're not; they're spirits having a physical experience.

The perfection within us is seeking expression all the time. That's why if we run, we want to run faster. If we jump, we want to jump higher. If we sell, we want to sell more. It doesn't matter what we do; we've got the desire to do more. We should understand why.

Creative Dissatisfaction

When I was a little boy, my grandmother used to tell me, "You should be satisfied with what you've got." Grandma was an angel, and we didn't want to say she was wrong, because how could Grandma be wrong? But she was.

We should never be satisfied with what we've got.

Dissatisfaction is a creative state, and by wanting more, you're going to do more, it's not a matter of getting it. If you think having more is going to make you better, you're kidding yourself. You're going to be miserably disappointed. It's *doing* more. You're going to bring more of yourself to the party. That's all I'm doing; I'm just bringing more of me to the surface. I want to do a better job today than I did yesterday.

The idea of retiring seems to indicate that the objective in life is to get enough to live on so you don't have to work. But we're not made for work; work is made for us. We get satisfaction from our work. You go to work for satisfaction. You earn money by providing service. You provide service to earn money.

We've got to get some of this straightened out. We've got it wrong, because people in powerful positions had it wrong, and they were teaching us, and we thought, how could they be wrong?

Corporations and Systems

Up to now I've been talking about individuals, but let's apply this idea to a larger framework, let's say a corporation. These principles are very important, but I don't think they're properly understood by people in key positions. We spend a lot of money on systems, on buildings, on things, but we don't spend that much on people.

Let's take a hotel as an example. When you take the people out of the hotel, you don't have a hotel anymore; you have a building full of stuff. The hotel is people. If we want to build a business, we've got to build the people.

Everybody has the potential. We've got to learn how to develop that potential. If you want a person to do a better job, you'd better find out what they want, because the only time they're really going to try to do better is when they're working towards something they really want. You've got to want something in order to bring more of yourself to the party.

We tell employees, "Listen, you've made a mistake. Let me show you how to do this right," but they go back to the way they've been doing the task, because they're programmed to do it that way. That's their paradigm, and telling them something isn't going to change it. They may change for today or tomorrow, but then boom! Right back to the paradigm.

The paradigm is like a thermostat: it controls the temperature of the person's performance. If you want to change the temperature of their performance, you've got to change the paradigm. You have to change that thermostat, and to do that you have to understand it. You have to start educating people so that they start to understand who they are, what they are, and what makes them tick.

I've gone into companies and taught these principles; the results have been astronomical. Way back in the seventies, I went into Prudential of America and Metropolitan, two of the largest insurance companies. We raised the sales by hundreds of millions of dollars by teaching the people to form a couple of new habits. I got people to commit to being in front of a prospect by 9:00 a.m. and asking them to purchase $100,000 worth of insurance. We told them, "You don't even have to sell it; just ask them to buy. The only two things you have to do differently are to be in front of somebody before 9:00 a.m. and ask them to purchase $100,000 in insurance." They were selling more $100,000 policies in a week then they had in a year.

I've gone into prison and seen the same thing happen. When you show a person why they're getting the results they're getting and what they have to do to change those results, there's a pretty good chance they're going to do it. If you're just trying to get them to change, they're not going to do it.

People don't resist change; they resist being changed. If you decide to change, you'll change. If I decide that you'll change and you didn't, you're going to resist my efforts. We've got to make it appealing to people to want to do better, to change, to be more productive. To do that, we have to understand what makes them tick. We have to understand how their mind functions. Understanding how the mind functions isn't just for psychologists. It's for everybody, because the mind is movement. The body is the manifestation of that movement.

There was a story about Mahatma Gandhi. Someone was coming through a huge crowd of people toward him and handed him a piece of paper saying, "Would you write down some profound idea message for me to take home?" Gandhi wrote down, "I am my message." If you are the leader, you have to operating at the vibrational level at which you hope the people around you will operate. You have to be living out your aims for your organization.

In the same way, if we want people in the organization to understand themselves, we've got to understand ourselves. We have to be studying with them.

The thing I enjoyed the most about working with Earl Nightingale was that he was forever studying. He studied all the time, and it was like Gandhi saying, "I am the message." Earl was the message.

I would watch what he was doing and what he studied. On one occasion, he had a book holder on his desk with a book by the early twentieth-century inspirational author Thomas Troward. It was opened to a certain page.

"What's significant about that?" I asked.

"I've been studying that for three months."

"Same page?"

"Yeah. When I understand it, I'll go to the next page."

I started doing that; I've got all of Troward's books, and I study them all the time. I started doing what Earl did. He was the message to me. I think that's what we've got to do. If we're going to lead people, we've got to do what we want them to do. There's no point in telling people to do something if you're not doing it yourself.

Understand Your Program

The paradigm is the most important concept that anyone can study. It controls everything in our lives. Now I think I've got a pretty good understanding of this concept, but I want to understand it better, so I keep studying more. If you want to change something, you've got to use repetition. If you'd only told been told your name once, you wouldn't even know what it is. They had to call you by name over and over until finally you started to respond to it.

A lot of the ideas that are controlling people right now are absurd, and they were originated by someone that may have lived maybe three or four hundred years ago, but they've been passed along in the DNA since then, and they've become part of your DNA. This kept expanding for about 280 days after conception until you made your debut on the planet. Your mind was wide open; everything that was going on around you went right into your subconscious mind.

Most people are starting out behind the eight ball. That's OK, because you can change that. I was twenty-six when I started to change; I've done fairly well, I've helped a few million people change, but I've still got a lot to learn.

I have been at it for a long time. I've gone into prisons, I've gone into schools, I've gone into corporations. The human being is a fascinating expression of life. We've got awesome powers locked up within us. If we're going to change, we've got to understand what's involved. If you're going to drive the car, you have to understand what the gearshift is for. You have to understand something about your computer if you're going to work with it. There are programs in our computer, and we rely on them. If we want to program change, we have it done by somebody that writes code.

Your paradigm is a program, and it's in your bio-computer. The people who wrote the code for the program controlling your life knew nothing about the mind. They were passing along what they had received. Nevertheless, they installed this program through repetition. We were taught the same things over and over: how to use a spoon, how to walk, how to get one foot in front of the other. It was repetition—patient, constant, spaced repetition.

Attitude: The Magic Word

Attitude is everything. How well anybody will do with this material will depend on their attitude, which is the composite of their thoughts, feelings, and actions. They're joined together like the colors of a rainbow.

I've listened to a record of Earl Nightingale's, which is a magnificent essay on attitude called *The Magic Word*, over and over, perhaps ten thousand times. The magic word is *attitude*. By repeatedly listening to this record, I became aware of what attitude is. Then I became aware of my own attitude. I became aware that I had a bad attitude about who I was and what I was capable of doing. I had to become aware, first, of what attitude actually is, and then I had to become aware of how to change it. I changed it the way it was built. Somebody else had built it through repetition. Because what Earl had to say about attitude went against everything I had been taught up to that point, I would listen to the same record over and over again.

I have a copy of Napoleon Hill's *Think and Grow Rich* bound in black leather. I've been reading this particular copy every day since 1963. I started reading this book when I was twenty-six. My sister Helen, two years older than me, had a friend named Pat, and Pat was a reader. She always had books; she always had a book with her. I think Pat read everything in the local library.

Think and Grow Rich was the first book I ever read.

When I was first given this book, I said, "I can't read." That wasn't true. I could not read well, but I could read, about as well as most people: at a seventh-grade level.

When I started to read this book, my sister said to Pat, "Bob started to read."

When I saw Pat, she asked, "Helen said you're reading?"

"Yes."

"What are you reading?"

"It's a good book. You'll enjoy it. *Think and Grow Rich*." She smiled.

A few months later, I saw Pat again. She asked, "Hey, Bob, are you still reading?"

"Yeah," I said.

"What are you reading?"

"*Think and Grow Rich*."

"Gee, you were into that last time I saw you."

"Yeah," I said, "I'm still reading it."

She looked at me kind of strangely.

A few months later, Pat asked me, "Are you still reading?"

"Yeah."

"What are you reading?"

"*Think and Grow Rich*."

I read that one book for a long time. I was doing what's required to change a paradigm. I didn't know that; I wasn't doing it deliberately; I was just fascinated with what I was reading.

Pat thought that was strange behavior. She'd read a book and then go on to another one. Pat was well educated, because she read so many books, but she didn't even know herself. She was a maintenance person, and she and her husband had nothing. They never got anywhere. They never accomplished anything in their lives. They just got by. God's highest form of creation, and they just got by.

As I often say in my seminars, "When you read a good book through the second time, you don't see something in that book that wasn't there before; you see something in *yourself* that wasn't there before." The repetition creates the awareness.

I'll give you another example of the necessity of repetition. When I was a kid, I had a friend named Jack Gregory. While we were hanging around his house, I would say, "Are youse coming?"

Jack's mother would say, "Bob, it's not *youse*, it's *you*."

I thought that she just didn't know that because there were more than one of them, it has to be *youse*. I tried to keep saying *youse*, and she kept correcting me.

Then I would hear somebody say, "Are you coming?" when they were talking about more than one person. I would hear somebody else say, "Are you coming?" in the same kind of context.

I would try correct myself. I'd start to say, "Are youse coming?" and I would stop myself and say, "Are *you* coming?" I felt very uncomfortable saying this, but eventually I changed my habit of speaking.

Now, whenever I ever hear anybody say *youse*, I immediately think of Mrs. Gregory. Mrs. Gregory used repetition to create an awareness in my mind. I don't think she knew she was doing that—I certainly didn't—but that's what she did.

That's what we have to do. We have to create awareness that what we're doing, our habitual behavior, is not producing the results we want. We have to become aware of how to change our behavior, and we have to change it the same way we have built it—through repetition.

Read the same book; listen to the same recording. If you listen to Earl's recording of *The Magic Word* for a couple of times a day for six months, I guarantee that you'll be acutely aware of your attitude, and although it sounds so simple, it will change your life. I still have my old record player and the little seven-inch records that Earl recorded way back in the early sixties. I still listen to them over and over again, because I know that I can have a better attitude than I have.

Chapter Two

Are You Living in Someone Else's Paradigm?

As I said in the previous chapter, very likely you are not living in a paradigm that you built yourself. Only on very rare occasions is a person is living with their own paradigm. Almost everyone has had their paradigm built for them—a parent, a guardian, someone else—and it controls their whole lives.

Create the World You Want

The subconscious mind, which operates according to your paradigm, is wide open, and everything that's going on around goes right into it. The subconscious mind is totally deductive. It has no originating capacity whatsoever. It is also amoral. It's like the earth, which really doesn't care what you plant in it. As Earl Nightingale said in *The Strangest Secret*, you can plant sweet corn, and a sixteenth of an inch away you can plant nightshade, a deadly poison. One will grow in just great abundance as the other.

So it is with the subconscious mind. Whatever you plant will grow. Like the earth, the subconscious doesn't determine what's good or bad; it just accepts and grows it. Your subconscious mind expresses itself through your actions.

Many seminars will have you sit down and write out how you would like to live, where you would like to live, what you would like to do, what you would like to earn, and whom you would you like to mix with. When you've written down all these things down in detail, you've built a picture.

For most people, that's usually the end of the exercise. Our imagination and our reason created that picture, but it's only through repetition that you're going to plant that idea in your subconscious mind. To do that, you have to write it out over and over again.

Three times every morning, I write out nine lines and record them. I send them to Sandy Gallagher, my business partner. She does the same; we're both on the same frequency. It's the way we want to see our business and what we want to accomplish with it. We reinforce this vision through repetition. We'll do this for a year or fourteen months. We're creating the world that we want to live in in our own company.

That's what has to be done. Writing causes thinking, and thinking creates pictures. You're creating an image in your consciousness with your imagination, and you're painting it with words to bring something beautiful about.

Once I asked an artist how he did such beautiful work. He said, "I dreamed my painting, and then I paint my dream." That's essentially what we're doing: we're dreaming our painting, and then we're going to paint our dream. Through the repetition of writing this vision over and over, we're planting it in universal intelligence via the subconscious.

The universal intelligence of the subconscious mind functions in a lawful way, and it works exactly the same way for everyone, whether you're living in the middle of Africa or the middle of Chicago. When you impress an idea over and over upon the subconscious, that idea must by law manifest through you. This process causes us to do things a little differently, because that idea has to be expressed.

Shortly after *The Secret* come out, I was getting on a plane, and a man got into the seat behind me. He reached over, and tapped me on the shoulder.

I smiled and said, "Well, who are you?"

He told me who he was. He was a golf pro, and he was going to the FedEx tournament in New York. He had just watched *The Secret* and said, "I think you can help me."

"I could probably help you a lot," I said.

One thing led to another, but essentially I told him how he had to fix the ideas in his subconscious mind in order to create a new paradigm.

That's really what you're doing. The paradigm is the picture that controls your behavior and gives you the results you want. You don't have to worry about where they're coming from: they'll come because you're in harmony with them.

Do You Want To?

Consider this: nothing is created or destroyed. All science and theology teach that. Everything is already here, in one state or another. People often have trouble making decisions because they don't know where the resources are going to come from to manifest them. I say, the only prerequisite to making a decision is, *do you want to?* The money, the help, the people—none of that is important. The only prerequisite when you're making a decision is, do you want to? What you want is on a frequency that's much higher than the one you're operating on. When you make a decision and you commit to it, you flip your mind into that frequency. You have to stay there; then it becomes part of your new paradigm. You've got to stay on that frequency, because it controls your behavior as well as what you attract to you. Our mind operates the same way as a radio or phone. You've got to get on the frequency of the good you desire.

I was around fifteen when my family got our first phone. It was a party line, shared by probably fifty people. Why did we have to have a party line? Because we weren't aware that there's an infinite number of frequencies. Once we became aware of that, everybody could have a phone. There are millions of phones because there's an infinite number of frequencies.

Your phone number is a frequency. In the mind, your paradigm is your frequency. The picture in the subconscious mind dictates the frequency we're on, what we're doing, and what's coming to us.

As I write this, there's a pandemic going on outside. It's a sad thing, but it's not going to slow me down. I'm working with the law, and I know everything I require is going to be attracted to me. It's going to come when I absolutely need it, not before—because that's the way the law works—so I must be patient and do what I have to do to stay on the same frequency.

Determined Imagination

I want more than I've got, not because I want more money, but because I want to grow. I want to become more aware of my oneness with infinite intelligence, with God. If we really understand this and keep working at it, it's going to happen, but we've got to keep working at it. We have to paint the picture of the good that we desire and write it down. When you have created an image in your conscious mind, you impress it on the subconscious mind through repetition, and you let yourself feel it. It's got to be real.

Neville called this "determined imagination." Thinking from the end is the beginning of all miracles. You don't work toward it; you go where you already are in your mind, and you get emotionally involved. Then it's only a period of time until it comes to pass on the physical level. You've got to live in the now. I've got it *now*: the second I see it in my mind, the second I get emotionally involved with it, I've got it.

Everybody's going to think you're a little crazy, but that's OK. They'll think so anyway. They don't know; they don't even know they don't know. You're moving ahead, and they're not, so they're going to think you're crazy; they're going to think you're making a mistake. The truth is, you're starting to do things the right way, but only a very small percent of the population is doing it the right way. About 95 percent are trying, but only 5 percent win.

A woman in Germany taught me something I think I knew intuitively but hadn't heard said in words. She said, "All success is 5 percent strategy, 95 percent mindset," and that's right.

We have been programmed, and part of our programming is to live from the outside in. We've been taught to live through our senses: "Will you *listen* to what I'm telling you? Will you *look* at what I'm showing you?" I have two little dogs in the house. They can see, hear, smell, taste, and touch, but they don't have the intellectual factors that I do: perception, will, reason, imagination, intuition, memory.

A-, B-, and C-type Goals

We also go about things the wrong way. I sort goals by ABC. A-type goals are doing what we already know how to do. Now goals are not for getting: getting is merely a by-product. Goals are for growing. Goals enable you to draw on this marvelous power that you've got locked up within you.

Once I asked a person in a seminar, "What is your goal?"

He said, "I want to get a new car."

"What kind of car do you want?" I asked.

"A Pontiac."

"What are you driving now?"

"A Pontiac."

"I see," I said. "How old is the car?"

"Four years old."

"How long have you had it?"

"Four years."

"What you're telling me, then, is, you got a new Pontiac four years ago, is that right?"

"Yeah."

"Then that's not a good goal. For four years, you've known how to get a new Pontiac, so there's no gain there. Now that doesn't mean you shouldn't get a new Pontiac, but that's not a good goal. For four years, you've already known how to get a new Pontiac. Going to the store to buy bread is not a goal, even though you're still going to do it, but there's no growth attached to it."

Then there is the B-type goal. A B-type goal is something a person thinks they can do: "If this person pays me what she owes me, and if this happens and that happens, I could actually do this." That's the B-type goal: you can see how to get there. If a whole bunch of conditions and circumstance and things happen in a certain way, you could do it.

The C-type goal involves something you have no idea how you're going to get. It's off in the dark. It's beyond anything you've ever done before, but it's what you want. It's the house you want. It's the job you want. It's the business you want. It's the accomplishment you want. You have no idea how to do it. You haven't got the money, you haven't got the time, and you don't have the wherewithal to make it happen, but you want it.

That is the only true prerequisite for a goal: you've got to really want it. Wants come from the essence of who we are, the perfection that's within us. That spiritual DNA, which is perfect, is motivating us, it's coming into our consciousness: "Want this."

I sat in a house on Maplewood Lane in Glenview, Illinois, in 1973. I'd just left working at the Nightingale-Conant Corporation. Except for my family, I was alone. I took my pen and said, "I'm going to build a company that operates all over the world." I had absolutely no idea how I was going to do it. I certainly didn't have enough money to pull it off. I didn't have any help and I didn't have any employees, but I had an idea.

As Andrew Carnegie said, any idea that's held in the mind and emphasized, whether feared or revered, will at once begin to clothe itself in the most convenient and appropriate form available. This reminds me of the great suffering of Job in the Bible. He said, "The thing which I greatly feared is come upon me" (Job 3:25). If you're afraid of something, you're going to attract it.

In any case, I had no idea how it would happen, but I wrote down, "I'm going to build a company that operates all over the world." Today we operate in eighty-nine different countries. I built a television station. We can broadcast all over the world. When we stream a seminar, we go into 119 countries.

That was the picture, and it's happened. Now we have some three thousand consultants that work with us. I want a hundred thousand. I'm a long way from my target, but I'm acting as if I'm already there, because I am there in my consciousness.

With the C-type goal, you're going where you've never been. Steve Jobs said, "You cannot connect the dots looking forward. You can only connect them looking backwards." You see how you got to where you are, but you can't see how you're going to get to where you're going. But if you hold the picture in your mind and you stay emotionally involved, it will reveal itself. Seek first this kingdom and its expansion in righteousness, and all these things will be given to you. You're going to attract everything that's necessary. If you hold the picture, everything you need will come to you when you need it, but not before.

Attract What You Need

Over fifteen years ago, I was doing a seminar in Vancouver, Washington. A woman came who was a securities attorney. She came because somebody had told her the seminar was a management program. It wasn't a management program at all; it was a "Science to Getting Rich" seminar. She fell in love with this information. This woman had a doctor's degree in law; she was buying and selling banks, turning banks public. She had gone to the best universities in America and in the U.K. She had graduated at the top of her class.

This woman fell in love with what we were doing. She bought everything we were selling. About three years later, she became my business partner. She owns half of this company. She is the Gallagher of the Proctor Gallagher Institute. Her genius has helped us grow. She understands money; I don't. I know how to get it, but I don't know how to manage it properly.

That's why we're growing so rapidly and doing so well: because I attracted what I needed. We've got a young guy who understands everything in the studio we built. He walked in from Manchester, England. He knows how to do everything; he could operate it on his phone from England if he wanted it to. I've got a creative director who has done all kind of television work. We've got one of the most phenomenal teams of people you've ever seen. All of them were attracted because of what I wrote down that day on Maplewood Lane in Glenview, Illinois, 1973.

Once I wrote down that goal, I started to work as if I'd already reached it, because that's what you've got to do. Neville said, "The future must become the present in the imagination of the one who would wisely and consciously create circumstances."

Neville also spoke of "thinking from the end." In other words, you don't work toward a goal; you're already there the second you've said it. Thinking from the end is an intense perception of the world of fulfilled desire. You've got to see yourself with what you want and act as if you've already got it. Build your paradigm as a picture of how you want to live your life. With every aspect of your life that you want to change, how do you want it to change; what do you want it to be like? Describe it in detail, and it's always got to be in the present tense. Begin everything by writing, "I am so happy and grateful now that . . ."

Some people worry about stretching too far. They say that your goal has to be anchored in at least a bit of reality, because if you overreach, you'll strain yourself. But reality is an interesting word; it's part of the paradigm. The Wright brothers were not realistic. I had the good fortune of working with Sir Edmund Hillary on two or three occasions. He's gone now, God bless him, but he certainly wasn't being realistic when he became the first man to climb Mount Everest. A lot of people have died trying to get to the top of that mountain.

I don't think there's any limit to what you're capable of doing. Nonetheless, it's true that if you stretch too much at the outset, you could cause yourself problems.

That's trying to force things. We don't know how long it takes to get in shape for running a marathon. We don't know how long it takes to get million dollars. We only know that we can get there. The time frame may be different for you than me.

Your new paradigm is an idea, and all seeds have a gestation period. For a human baby, it's about 280 days. In Canada, where I live, it's around seventy days for a carrot. We don't know what this gestation period is for a spiritual seed, which is an idea; no one knows what the gestation period is for an idea. You guess at the time, but you're guessing, and you'll usually guess wrong. Now I have known a couple of people who guessed right and landed on the exact day they had visualized, but that's unusual. Even so, I don't think there's any limit to what we can do, because you're working with infinite intelligence and with the law by which how everything happens. Everything happens by law, and when they go wrong, we're violating the law.

Create or Disintegrate

The Bible says, "The wages of sin is death" (Romans 6:23). When I heard that as a kid, I thought, "Whoa! Is that ever severe!"

Is that true? Yes. I just didn't understand what "death" meant here. There's a basic law of life that says, create or disintegrate. If you're not going ahead, you're going backwards. When you violate the law, that's the sin. You go backwards; you're working against it; you're trying to force things. When you're working with the law, you go ahead. When you're doing it right, everything flows beautifully. If you have to really struggle, you're probably going against the law.

At one point I was working with a multimillion-dollar company on a program. I like the individual involved, and he likes me, but what we were trying to do was too much of a struggle. I knew it right then and told him that I thought we should forget it, because we were struggling. "I think we're working against the law," I said. "I think there's something wrong with what we're doing. I don't know what it is, but I think you'll agree with me. There's a struggle, and there shouldn't be; it should be a free flow." When things are clicking along for you, you're doing it right; you're doing it by law.

Science-fiction author Robert A. Heinlein once observed, "In the absence of clearly defined goals, we become strangely loyal to performing daily trivia until we ultimately become enslaved by it." I relate that quote to the situation of a new baby. The baby has been inundated with trivia—the conversations that are going on around the baby, things that are deemed to be important, worrying about this, worrying about that: "What if this happens? What if that happens?" All of this trivia ultimately enslaves the baby. It becomes part of the baby's paradigm. That does a great deal of damage.

Find Your Purpose

We've got to have a purpose to our lives—a reason for getting out of bed. When you have a purpose in life and you're being guided by it, all this trivia will just bounce off like water from a duck, because you're not in harmony with any of it.

Futurist Joel Barker, who wrote a book called *Paradigms*, said that in order to shape your future, you have to be willing and able to change your paradigm. Willing is very important, but if you don't have purpose, the odds are pretty good that you won't be willing, because you have to do things that don't make a whole lot of sense to you at first. You've got to start doing things that go against your paradigm.

For example, part of my paradigm is to be in my studio at 5:30 a.m. and do my writing exercises. The last thing I do is write ten things I'm grateful for, and I do this every day. It's not difficult for me; it would be difficult now if I didn't do it, because it's part of my paradigm now. But when you first start doing these things, you're not only forming a new habit, you're breaking an old one, and that's not an easy thing to do. That's why people on weight loss programs have a difficult time: they're not only forming new habits but breaking old ones. If you don't have a strong sense of purpose, you probably won't be willing to do that.

You've got to have a purpose that really means something: it's the reason you get out of bed in the morning. We're not here just to earn enough to get by. Your purpose then makes you willing to pay the price to do it; and without the purpose, you won't do that.

How do you decide on the purpose? That takes some discipline in itself. You could start by sitting down and asking yourself, "What do I really love doing?" I believe we're all hardwired to do something really well. I'm really good at what I do. I'm not much good at anything else, but I don't want to do anything else. I just work at getting better at what I'm doing.

I recommend doing the following exercise early in the morning. I'm more creative in the morning. That's why doctors operate early in the morning: their hand is steady, and the patient is more receptive. Sit down in the morning and ask yourself, "What do I really love doing?" I think you'll find your purpose there. It's your purpose because you love it.

You can easily get on the wrong track here. When I was speaking at a seminar in Phoenix, a doctor told me he was thinking of leaving his profession.

"Why is that?" I asked. "You can earn enough money."

"Today," he said, "the medical profession is all messed up. You've got to work harder and put in more time to earn less money."

"That's probably true," I said, "but why did you become a doctor in the first place?"

"Because I love it."

"You'd better think about what you're doing, then, because if you love it, it doesn't make any difference whether you're getting paid or not. You're spending your days doing what you love to do. You don't go to work to earn money; you go to work for satisfaction. You provide service to earn money." I explained that to him until he finally got it.

Desire: The Key to Ability

Anyone can do what anyone else has done. I don't think there's any limit to what you're capable of doing, but it's strongly linked to desire. If you aren't able to play football like Tom Brady, you won't want to play football like Tom Brady. Napoleon Hill said, "If you have the desire, you'll have the ability to do it. If you don't have the desire, you won't have the ability. The ability comes with the desire."

So you could be a poor boy or girl living in a poor neighborhood, but you really desire to have a few million dollars in the bank. You could do that, even if you don't desire to have the money of a Jeff Bezos.

If you have the desire, you have the ability. Don't question how it's going to happen, because you won't know that until after it happens. Hillary did not know how to get to the top of Mount Everest until after he got there. The Wright brothers didn't know how to get the plane in the air until after they did.

The way will be shown, but you've got to get on the frequency of the good that you desire. Most people are on an AM frequency but wishing they had FM music. If you want FM music, you've got to get on the FM frequency.

If you want an example of someone who was living someone else's paradigm but turned it around, you can take my own life. At twenty-six, I was underweight, I was shy, I had very low self-esteem, I owed money to everybody I knew, and I had never done anything of any consequence. I was kicked out of school after two months in high school, and I wasn't a very nice person. I had a bad attitude.

Today I think I'm a very nice person. I've earned millions of dollars, I've helped millions of people, I'm at the top of my game. I don't know anybody that is doing what I'm doing better than I am. And I believe that if I could go and do it, anybody can.

Out of Solitary

For years, I was going into Kingston Penitentiary, a maximum security prison in Canada, once a month. I had a deal cut with the security people. I said, "Anybody that wants to come and listen to me should be able to come."

"Oh," they said, "that's being ridiculous."

"No, it's not," I said, "If anybody wants to come, they've got to be able to come." Finally they agreed.

There was one guy who'd been in solitary confinement for seven and a half years. He had shot someone in a hold-up near Windsor, Ontario. The guy didn't die. If he had, they would've hanged this man, because at that time they were hanging people in Canada for murder. He was sentenced to twenty-seven years. He had been in solitary confinement for seven and a half years; he got out one hour a day by himself in the yard. The warden called him a mad dog. He was a big guy: six feet two, two hundred pounds.

When I started teaching this information, this man would come in and sit in the back. I'd brought in cigarettes, coffee, and doughnuts. He was sitting in the back, eating doughnuts, smoking, and drinking coffee, making noises like an animal, sitting on a table with his legs swinging. If I said something about faith, he'd laugh and scoff. He was getting everybody's attention. This went on for about three months. I knew that I either had to stop it or quit going there.

I didn't want to quit going, but I was scared of this guy. Then one day, when he started to act up, I stopped what I was doing and very slowly walked to the back. I stood right in front of him and said, "You've got to be the stupidest bastard I've ever met." You could see his muscles tighten up, and his face went red; I thought he was going to kill me. Then he started to laugh; he must have thought, "This guy is crazy." All of this happened in seconds, milliseconds.

"I can earn money faster than you can steal it," I said. "In half an hour, I'm going to tell the security to open the door. I'm going to go out, get in a nice car, and drive away from here. You're going back in a cell for another twenty hours." He was quiet then.

The next month he was sitting in the front, and if anybody shuffled their feet, he turned and glared at them; he was like the disciplinary officer in my meeting.

Eventually, they let this prisoner out on a special parole. He had been married with two sons, and while he was in prison, his wife had a little girl. He was befriended by a priest, who arranged for his wife to get back together with him. He couldn't leave the city of Toronto, and he had to report to the Mounties every month and to the city police every week.

This guy came to work with me. A year or so after, I went down hammering on the desk of the parole office, saying, "You've got no right keeping this guy on parole. I'm going to England, and I want to take him with me."

They tore up his parole and gave him his passport, and off he went. Never got in trouble again. Lived a good life. He's gone now, but he was worth all kinds of money when he died. If this worked for him, it can work for anybody.

The Learners Shall Inherit the Earth

At a human resources congress held in 1969 by the Nightingale-Conant Corporation, we had philosopher Eric Hoffer as a speaker. He was a grand man. He never went to school, and he worked as a longshoreman, but he was a very confident human being. Hoffer wrote a number of books, the greatest of which was *The True Believer*. At our congress, he said, "In times of change, the learners will inherit the earth. While the learned find themselves beautifully equipped to deal with a world that no longer exists, the learners will inherit the earth."

I took that to mean people that are continually studying are going to be happy, healthy, and wealthy. Actually, there is no such thing as a learned person. You're either learning or you're not.

Hoffer also said, "To learn, you need a certain degree of confidence—not too much, not too little. If you have too little confidence, you'll think you can't learn. If you have too much, you'll think you don't have to learn."

It's very important to have a certain degree of confidence all the time so that we'll continue to grow, expand, and learn about ourselves, the world that we're a part of, and what we're capable of doing. I'll talk about this in the next chapter.

Chapter Three

Developing the Confidence to Change Your Paradigm

*I*n the last chapter I mentioned a human resources congress that featured Eric Hoffer. I was in the back of the ballroom at the same congress, at the O'Hare Hyatt in 1969, when Bill Gove was speaking. There were about a thousand people in the audience. He stood in front of them with had a handheld mic, and he said, "If I want to be free, I've got to be me. Not the me I think you think I should be, not the me I think my wife thinks I should be, not the me I think my kids think I should be. If I want to be free, I've got to be me." He added, "I'd better know who me is."

He had his audience right in the palm of his hand. Now I had gathered a ton of information, and I'd been studying it every day for about eight years. I was standing in the back corner of the room and thinking, "Wow, he's so good! If only I could do that!"

On his *Magic Word* recording, Earl Nightingale says, "Now right here we come to a rather strange point. We tend to minimize the things we can do and the goals we can accomplish, and for some equally strange reason, we think other people can accomplish things that we cannot." He added, "I want you to understand that's not true, that you've a got deep pool of talent and ability within you."

If, at that 1969 conference, you were to ask me, "Do you understand what Earl said?" I'd have said, "Of course I understand it. I've been listening to this straight for nine years every day." But all of a sudden it was as if a rocket had gone off my mind: "That's what Earl means." I was thinking I couldn't do what Bill Gove was doing. At that point I made up my mind that not only was I was going to do what he was doing, I was going to get him to teach me. I made up my mind to leave a note for Bill Gove asking him to teach me how to do what he was doing. I was ready to learn.

Confidence Comes from Knowledge

Confidence comes from knowledge. When people say they don't have any confidence, that's not completely true. They're probably confident that they can get dressed, tie their shoes, and drive a car. They're confident that they can do all kinds of things. When they don't have the confidence to do something they'd really like to do, it's because they don't know how. The more you learn how, the more confidence you'll have.

I made up my mind I would learn how to do what Gove was doing, so I got to know him and paid him thousands of dollars on a number of occasions to sit down with him. I don't speak like Bill Gove at all. He would never know that he was the one who taught me to speak. I had the ability to speak inside of me. He didn't need to teach me that. He taught me how to be calm and confident in front of a group of people. He said, "Quit worrying about what they think of you." That's what I really learned. Author Terry Cole-Whittaker wrote a book called *What You Think of Me Is None of My Business*. That's the way it is.

The Tyranny of "Other People"

That brings me to a related issue: the tyranny of "what other people will think." Earl Nightingale helped me there. He said, "If you knew how little other people were thinking, you wouldn't be concerned with what they're thinking." If the average person said what they were thinking, they would be speechless. Dr. Ken McFarland, a great educator down in Kentucky, said, "Two percent of the people think, three percent think they think, and ninety-five percent would actually rather die than think."

What you think of yourself is very important. What other people think of you is not important. I used to be very concerned with what other people thought of me; I'm not anymore, because I realize what somebody else thinks of me really has no bearing on my life. What *I* think of me is everything. If I really work at being a nice person and I work at accomplishing something, other people will probably like me, but if I go around concerning myself with what other people think, I'm not going to accomplish very much.

Bill Gove taught me to be relaxed in front of an audience. He said, "Remember: you're only talking to one person. You could have a whole room full of people, but there's only one person. You've got to get that straight in your head and be really interested in sharing something of value with the person that is listening."

If you focus your attention on what *you* think of you, everything will work out pretty well. That's what I've done, and that's the way it's worked out. At this writing, I'm eighty-six, and hopefully I will grow for another ten years, but I know right now things are going very well. I like me; I like what I'm doing and how I'm doing it.

A lot of this worrying about what other people think starts early in life. When we were little kids, we would hear our parents say, "What would the neighbors think?" I've come to this conclusion: hopefully the neighbors do think, but what they think really doesn't make any difference. Most people are concerned with what other people think. They shouldn't be. They should be concerned with what they think of themselves.

We've got to take a look at how we're living. Are we choosing our own path? Are we operating on an image of the kind of life we want and execute it, or are we just trying to get by as best we can day to day?

You've got to know where you are. Furthermore, you have to know where you're going. Earl Nightingale's definition of success is the best I've ever heard: "Success is the progressive realization of a worthy ideal." An ideal is an idea that you've fallen in love with. You are progressively becoming aware as you're moving towards the good you desire.

Money: A Necessary Commodity

Not everyone may want to create wealth, but everyone, I believe, should put themselves in a solid financial position, since money is used for other people's products or services. It's a necessary commodity in the world we live in. Everyone can create that kind of wealth.

Once I was flying on a plane to Kuala Lumpur from Toronto. It's twenty-five hours in the air one way, so I had a lot of time to think. I spent the time doodling on a pad with a calculator. I kept thinking, how can I improve the business? How can I create a new idea? I wrote down "$1,000,000"—the numeral 1 followed by six zeros. I had earned a million in the sixties, but I really didn't know what I had done. As I said earlier, I was unconsciously confident.

Then I thought of people I knew that had earned $1 million. What was so different about them? I suddenly realized they weren't different at all. It's that they didn't have just one source of income. If you have a job, you've got one source of income. I don't care how good you are at it, and I don't care how much you earn an hour, you still have only one source of income. Wealthy people have many sources. Historically, even if you go back to the ancient Babylonians, wealthy people all had multiple sources of income.

Then I got an idea. I would do a seminar to teach people how to earn $1 million by creating multiple sources of income. We did that very well—teaching how anybody could become wealthy by setting up multiple sources of income. You don't have one source; you have all kinds of them.

I have no desire to be as wealthy as Jeff Bezos. I have no desire to have millions of dollars; I'm happy with two or three million in the bank and being busy working and creating work, because I like to give it away and I like to do a lot of good. That's what I think wealth is for.

But anyone—I don't care who it is—can become reasonably wealthy, and it's easier today than it's ever been because of the Internet. I set up a company called MSI Connect. MSI stands for *multiple sources of income* or *multiple streams of income*, where people work together, helping one another set up their MSIs, doing joint ventures, and becoming affiliates.

There are many different places where people can go, but it's a matter of changing your paradigm. If you're not too interested in earning money, you should get interested, because it controls a good part of your life. If you're not interested, it's because your paradigm is trying to stop you. It's like a cop: it stands there and won't let you go past. You've got to get past that cop. You've got to decide that that paradigm is not going to control you anymore. Say, "No more. I'm moving ahead, I'm going ahead, and I'm not going to stop."

How much money do you want to earn? Get busy and start earning it. When I first started reading *Think and Grow Rich*, I went from earning $4,000 a year and I owed $6,000, so if I paid debt for a year and a half, I would have just broken even with nothing to live on.

In less than a year, my income had gone up to $14,500 a month. Somebody had said there was good money in cleaning floors. I said, "I'm not proud. I'll clean floors." I started to clean offices. We ended up cleaning them in seven cities and three different countries. Boom! Away it went.

You've got to get with people that know how to earn money; they will teach you how. It's a subject, and it has to be learned. School does not teach us how to earn money. A person could have a master's degree in commerce and finance and still be broke because they have never learned how to earn money. They may have learned how to keep it and count it, but they need to learn how to earn it.

Lloyd Conant and Earl Nightingale didn't start a business; they started an industry. I was having dinner at Lloyd's house in 1968 and I asked him how he started this company. He said, "I read a little green book all weekend. I wasn't interested in how he started the company anymore. I wanted to know what the green book was. It was *The Science of Getting Rich*, by Wallace D. Wattles, first published in 1910. Earl gave me a copy. I've never stopped reading it; it's phenomenal.

Success and the Worthy Ideal

Let me go back to Earl Nightingale's definition of success: "a progressive realization of a worthy ideal." Say someone has accumulated $5 million and is working towards $10 million. Another person is a student in school who's getting a C and D average but is working toward an A and B average. They're progressively moving in a given direction. Although their paths are totally different, one is equally as successful as the other because both are moving toward a predetermined objective.

Success is not where you are, it's where you're going. It's the direction you're moving in, your life aim. The basic law of life is, create or disintegrate. If you're working toward a predetermined goal, you're creating; you're doing what God meant you to do. I believe we're here to do God's work. Now they say God's the creator, so God's work would be creation. When we're given creative faculties, we should get on with the job and start creating, because we're quite capable of it.

A lot of people carry around the idea that they'll succeed if they just set a goal, write it down on an index card, and work as hard as possible. They're not going to go anywhere. They'll go up and down until they get tired of going up and down; then they'll quit and level out where they are, and that's the way they'll live the rest of their lives. Take the gyms and workout centers. People who own them have earned millions selling memberships. They know that when a person buys a year's membership, they may go for two or three weeks; then they'll stop going.

That's because the person never changed their paradigm. They want to change their body, but they don't want to change the thing that controls the body. The body is the instrument of the mind: it will reflect the operations of the mind, whether they are automatic or consciously and deliberately chosen.

If you understand the laws and you're working in harmony with them, you'll still have to work to reach your goal: it won't be just a walk in the park, but it's going to be a very good trip. You're going to enjoy it, and you're going to keep moving ahead.

But understand that moving ahead means that you're changing the paradigm. You want to change the results, but the results are nothing but the manifestation of your actions. Your actions are caused by the paradigm, not by how much you know. People know how to do better, but they don't do it.

We've got to change the paradigm if we're going to reach our goals. It's an absolute essential. No one who hasn't got some understanding of the paradigm is really going to enjoy a successful life—and oddly enough not many people understand the paradigm. Over the years, I've discovered that a lot of people are very successful but don't understand why. They have built a very good paradigm, but they don't have the satisfaction of knowing why they're doing well. What they've got is nontransferable: they can't give it to anybody else.

When you understand paradigms, you understand how they're built, and you understand how they can be changed. Then you're off to the races, because you can take control of your life. I've seen some beautiful things happening in people's lives when they understand these principles.

It doesn't matter what happened in the past or where you're starting. What matters is where you're going. When I started, I had a bad work record and a bad attitude, with nothing going for me. But none of that mattered. As it says in the Bible, "Let the dead bury the dead." That's good advice for dealing with the past.

First of all, you have to take into consideration that you do have a paradigm. I've got one, you've got one, and the paradigm dictates how well I'm going to do today, tomorrow, and in the near future. If I want to do better than what I've been doing I'm going to have to change the paradigms. I'm on a constant educational process of changing my own paradigm, improving it.

The paradigm is your habitual way of living. Part of your paradigm is very good: it serves you, it's good for you, it's good for other people, and it's creating good in your life. So a paradigm is not all negative, it's both positive and negative. I want to turn more of the bad ideas that I've got into good ideas and my bad habits into good habits, so I work at that every day, and I probably will until I die.

I went away for about three days with a couple of friends, and I worked on my purpose. I determined that my purpose is to live and work in a prosperous environment that encourages productivity and pleasure so that I can improve the service I render to my family, my community, my company, my nation, and ultimately the world. It's one of service.

It took me over three days to figure this out. You should spend time working out your purpose. It's your reason for getting out of bed, and it will help you make a lot of decisions. People offer me great opportunities, which could earn a lot of money. I'm not remotely interested in some of them, because they're off purpose.

Marshall Fields said, "Real estate is the best, safest way to become wealthy." I don't necessarily agree with that. A lot of money is earned in real estate, but I'm not remotely interested in real estate. That would be off track for me.

My purpose is what I'm doing: to live and work in a prosperous environment that encourages productivity and pleasure so that I can improve the service I render to my family, my company, my community, my nation, and ultimately the world. That's what I do. I do it every day, from early in the morning until early evening.

If you have not found your purpose, I would recommend setting aside ten to fifteen minutes every morning. Put a pen and pad someplace where you can sit quietly.

If you drink coffee, make yourself a cup of coffee, go to your spot, sit there, and ask, "What do I love doing?"

I believe we're all hardwired to do something great with our lives. We've been given enormous talent and ability—beyond the scope of our imagination. But if we don't find our purpose, we won't use this ability. We could end up running from one successful venture to another, remaining constantly frustrated, because it's never what we wanted and we don't get enough satisfaction from it.

Earl Nightingale said, "You don't go to work for money. You go to work for satisfaction. You provide service to earn money." If you're on purpose, you're going to get tremendous satisfaction from how you spend your days. I do, because everything I do is on purpose.

You may wonder whether your purpose is created or discovered. I believe it is discovered. One time I watched a woman who was being interviewed on television. She had been a dancer in a chorus line in Las Vegas, and she said, "I knew I wasn't a good enough dancer to be a star, so I quit. I loved baking pastry, so I moved to France, and I got jobs working with some of the best pastry shops in France." She became one of the best pastry chefs in the world.

At this point, you may be thinking, "But I can't earn any money doing what I love." It doesn't matter whether you're earning money if you love what you do. What matters is, do you love it?

Earl Nightingale also used to say that riches come in two forms: tangible and what he called "psychic." Psychic income is the satisfaction you get from the way you spend your days. Material income, of course, is the amount of money you earn. It's all based on the law of compensation, what Earl called the *formula*. The income you earn is in direct ratio to the need for what you do, your ability to do it, and the difficulty of replacing you. There's got to be a tremendous need for what you're doing, so you're going to get really good at it, and you're going to be really difficult to replace.

Chapter Four

Paradigms and Cybernetics

*Setting your Control System to
Achieve Your Desired Results*

*L*et me go on to the relation of paradigms to cybernetics. They're very similar. Cybernetics was discovered during World War II by Norbert Weiner and Arturo Rosenbluth, a mathematician and a physician respectively. It's the science of control and communication in the animal and some machines.

The best way to understand the cybernetic mechanism is with your thermostat. You will set the thermostat in your home to control the temperature of the house, let's say, to seventy degrees. I live in the north, where it gets very cold in the wintertime. You could be sitting and all of a sudden feel a cold draft around your feet, and the house is cold. You go to look at that thermostat and the temperature has dropped down to sixty-six degrees, and you wonder what's the matter. You find that somebody left the door open.

A message goes from the thermostat to the furnace. A fire's turned on, the fan is turned on, and it blows heat into the house until the thermostat gets up to seventy degrees, and then it shuts it all down.

The automatic pilot on the plane is a cybernetic mechanism. When the plane leaves its point of origin, the pilot will flip on the automatic pilot, that is, the cybernetic mechanism. Now he could go back and have dinner with you. He doesn't, but he could, because the automatic pilot is flying the plane. The plane may be hit by some unexpected turbulence that knocks it off course. The cybernetic mechanism cuts in and brings it back on course. It's always a matter of correcting and bringing the plane back on course. A cosmetic surgeon named Maxwell Maltz applied this concept to the mind in a book he published in 1960 called *Psycho-Cybernetics*.

A Psychological Mechanism

A paradigm is like a cybernetic mechanism. Suppose a person is seventy pounds overweight and wants to lose weight. They've got to stick to a diet. They start on the diet and, sure enough, stick to it. They lose five pounds, then seven, then ten.

Then the person starts eating the food they're not supposed to eat. What happened? The paradigm kicked in and took them back on their usual course. A diet is the start of writing a new paradigm, but people don't see it that way. Because they don't know how to write a new paradigm, they don't really understand the force that they're up against when they try to change their eating habits. Nine out of ten of them fail.

That's why people keep going on and off diets. When they start to lose weight, they're brought back on their usual course, and they'll keep eating until they get up to being seventy pounds overweight again. The paradigm works exactly the same as the thermostat or the automatic pilot. It controls your behavioral patterns. It controls what you're eating, your exercise, or whatever you're doing.

That person has to understand how the paradigm is controlling what they're eating. That's why diets do not work: people don't understand they're being controlled by this program and their subconscious mind. They're trying to fight the program without understanding what they're fighting. They're dealing with an unseen enemy, and that's very difficult.

When people start to understand how their mind functions, they can start making headway, because they've realized something about the enemy. The enemy is the paradigm. When they don't understand that fact, they feel as if they're failing, because they're not doing what they want to do. They give themselves a command, but they can't follow it.

Understanding Paradigms

Discipline is a big part of the solution. Discipline is the ability to give yourself a command and follow it. But for a person to be successful in disciplining themselves, they have to understand what they're working with. They have to understand what paradigms are and what they're doing. If they don't, they're in trouble, because they're fighting an unseen enemy.

King Solomon said, "With all thy getting, get understanding" (Proverbs 4:7). Understanding is the opposite of doubt and worry. Understanding how paradigms control us changes the game completely.

I have made a lot more headway since I started to understand why I had changed. When I was living in England, I was doing very well, but I didn't know why. I was unconsciously confident. I asked, "What happened?" I did not believe in a capricious God on a cloud who said, "Let Bob have a turn." I didn't believe in luck. Voltaire said, "Luck is word we invented to express the effects of unknown causes," so I didn't believe that God had singled me out to be lucky. I wanted to know what the hell happened. Why did I go from losing, losing, losing up until I was twenty-six, and then suddenly had tremendous success almost overnight?

When a person understands what a paradigm is and how it's controlling them, they're going to go on a diet and they're going to start eating properly. They're going to start controlling their body, because they see the body as an instrument of the mind: it obeys the operations of the mind. In his book *As a Man Thinketh*, James Allen wrote. "The body is a delicate and plastic instrument, which responds readily to the thoughts by which it is impressed, and habits of thought will produce their own effects, good or bad, upon it."

If you don't understand these principles, you'll have a hard time taking control and disciplining yourself, because you don't even know what you're fighting. When you understand what you're fighting, using a combination of discipline and desire, you're going to win.

Polarities

Put your left hand out, and put your right hand out. The left hand is one side; the right hand is the other. There's a law called the law of polarity. It is the law of opposites. Everything has an opposite: left, right; hot, cold; up, down; in, out. Let's say that the left is the negative: ignorance. On the right-hand side is the positive: knowledge. On the conscious level, ignorance is the cause of doubt and worry. When you internalize these things, you set up a vibration called *fear*. When that fear is expressed— and it must be expressed because it was impressed by the mind—it expresses itself in the body as anxiety. That's what anxiety is: the expression of the fear caused by doubt and worry. And the doubt and worry were caused by ignorance.

On the other hand is understanding. How do you get understanding? There's only one way: through study. You must study. Understanding leads to faith, which is the opposite of fear. Faith expresses itself in well-being rather than anxiety. Well-being is expressed as exhilaration.

Now in between doubt and worry on one hand and understanding on the other is *is*. It just *is*. Nothing is bad or good, right or wrong, except our thinking makes it so. Everything just *is*. Our thinking determines whether it's good or bad.

I think people should study. It's vitally important to study. But if we don't have a purpose and we don't have goals, we won't study; we get out of school, and we think we're finished. Unfortunately, school really never taught us how to study or what to study.

All this said, what things will really work in engraving the new paradigm in the subconscious? To begin with, I think a person has to understand that personal development does not have a finish line. We're used to studying something and finishing it. You never finish studying this material. You'll never know yourself as well as you want to. You're always going to be changing the paradigm. Your results are always under construction.

Growth and Discomfort

I'm at the point where I know that when I go after something new, it's going to cause discomfort. If I'm feeling really comfortable, I know there's no growth being experienced; I'm stuck. The difference is understanding what's happening versus not understanding. When you try to change a paradigm, you don't know what you're doing. The odds are pretty good that you're going to lose; the paradigm is going to win every time. That's why people have trouble with diets or saving money or moving ahead at work: they don't understand how the paradigm is formed and how it's controlling them. When you do understand, you never stop changing the paradigm. The potential is perfection. I know a couple of people who think they're perfect—they're pretty dull to be around—but no one is. Yet the potential is perfection.

You will be able to walk across the pool one day. I keep sinking, but the possibility is there. All things are possible.

When you truly understand that concept, you're always going to move into an uncomfortable situation, because you're always going where you've never been. You're improving your situation. You've got to know that that's what's happening. When I go after new goals, I know it's going to cause some discomfort, and you can get very tempted. I could sit back and coast until the end of my life. I could be very comfortable, but I would probably be very miserable, because I'm too aware of what's happening. I've got to keep growing.

Personal development is a never-ending process. Actually, personal development is a relatively new subject. Earl Nightingale and Lloyd Conant turned it into a business and helped people become more aware of it. Other people were fooling around in this area, but Earl and Lloyd took a very serious, businesslike approach. They attracted a lot of good people and built a company. People started to use the material the way it was meant to be used, and they started to see that these ideas works in companies as well as individually. So companies started to utilize this material.

When I was at Nightingale-Conant, from 1968 to 1973, there was no talk about paradigms. We referred to them as *subconscious conditioning*, but we didn't really understand its depth or how it was formed. After Joel Barker came out with his book *Paradigms* in 1993, we really got into the concept.

Earl Nightingale also talked about "constructive discontent": you're always wanting to improve, always moving forward. It's constructive, but at the same time it's discontent. You're not going to be comfortable, but you're happy because you know you're doing what you want and you're going in the direction that you want to go in.

Think from the State Desired

When people think of the intellect, they think of left-brain, logical functions, whereas the things that impress the subconscious are more oriented toward the right brain: affirming a goal with great emotion, and creatively visualizing that goal in ways that impress it visually on the mind. These practices help shift the paradigm.

Neville brought this point out in his book *The Power of Awareness*. He spoke of "thinking from the state desired"—in other words, seeing yourself already there. That's your imagination; that's the right-brain function. Thinking from the state desired is creative living. Ignorance of this ability to think from the end is bondage.

People who are very left-brain oriented, who went into law, engineering, or accounting, sometimes have a difficult time with this practice, but when they get it, they really get it, because left-brain people are very determined. Right-brain people are more fluid. They operate more through vibrations and feelings than through concepts.

One thing that stops many people from changing their paradigm is logic. But take a look at all the great breakthroughs, such as Hillary climbing Mount Everest with Tenzing Norgay. Nobody had ever done that before. Hillary had to do what was totally illogical. The same with the Wright brothers: it was totally illogical to believe that anything heavier than air was going to stay up there. They were totally illogical, but they did it. In every great breakthrough, people defied logic.

People say, you've got to be realistic. No, don't be realistic. When I'm setting a goal, I don't want to be realistic. I want to be totally illogical. I have problems about this with people in our own company from time to time, (although they're getting more used to me). If something is practical, I don't want to do it. I want to do something totally illogical.

For me to sit in my den and say, "I'm going to build a company that operates all over the world"—that was totally ridiculous. I didn't have enough money to pull something like that off. I had no idea what I was going to have to do, but I knew I would do it.

Hillary knew that he'd get to the top of Everest. He went in 1951 and failed. He went again in 1952 and failed. He had to go back in 1953. For three years in a row he went at it. The guy was a beekeeper from Auckland, New Zealand. People had died up there. When he said, "I'm going back again" in 1952, everybody got angry with him: "You've got no right doing that. You have responsibilities." The Wright brothers' father was a bishop in a very conservative denomination, and he told them they were going to burn in hell for suggesting they could fly.

All the great breakthroughs have been totally illogical. If you really want to live up to your potential and you're not trying to please everybody and his brother, set some goals that scare the daylights out of you. If you know you're going there and you're working in harmony with the law, you know it has to happen. It doesn't always happen when you want it to or when you think you need it. But you know it has to, because you're on that frequency.

When you get on the frequency of the good you desire, it's got to become your new home; it becomes the place from which you see the world. You're the only one who's gone there—not your wife, not your kids, not the next-door neighbor, not the people you work with. Consequently, you're going to see things they're not able to see.

If you're really going to live up to your potential, you've got to step out and really bet on *you*. I'm firmly convinced that we've got the potential to do anything that our imagination will show us. As Neville said, "Determined imagination, thinking from the end, is the beginning of the all miracles."

There's no such thing as miracles. Everything happens by law. There are only things that happen which we don't understand. If you accept the idea of miracles or luck, or of a capricious God that blesses some and curses others, you won't fly anywhere.

Chapter Five

How Your Beliefs Affect Your Paradigm

*M*ost people think of beliefs as something static and inherent. In other words, "This is what I believe, and I believe that for life. It's who I am." In the political context, people say, "I'm liberal or I'm conservative." In terms of their personality, they'll say, "I'm mild-mannered" or "I'm a type A person." "I believe men are good at X, and women are good at Y."

That's the way most people are, but it's not the way they should be, because our beliefs shape everything in our life. Our paradigm is made up of our beliefs. Unfortunately, many of the beliefs that we operate with are absolutely ridiculous. They have no foundation at all. In the light of truth, they would just disappear. Furthermore, we did not originate most of these silly beliefs.

Belief is a very interesting word. It played a big role in my life. I was trying to figure out why I was winning. I couldn't get anybody to answer me, to really tell me why. I knew that there were only two sources of reference: science and theology. I got into the various religions. I read the Qur'an, the Torah, the Bible, the Book of Mormon. It didn't matter where I went; everywhere it said, you've got to believe. William James at Harvard, way back in 1900, said, "Believe, and your belief will create the fact." But I wondered, "How do you believe it?"

I didn't know the answer to that. How do you change your belief? Why do I believe what I believe? One thing led to another. This went on for a few years. I could not figure it out and I couldn't get anybody to answer it.

Belief and Reevaluation

One day I was having a meal with Val Vanderwall, who was a mentor of mine. In idle conversation, he said, "Our belief system is based upon our evaluation of something. And frequently, if we reevaluate a situation, our belief about that situation will change."

When he said that, it was as if bells had gone off in my head, and I said, "Wait a minute. What did you just say?"

I had him repeat it: "Our belief system is based upon our evaluation of something. And frequently, if we reevaluate a situation, our belief about that situation will change."

It suddenly dawned on me. All of a sudden, I knew why and how my life had changed. I knew everything that I was looking for. With all of the records that I played and the books that I read, I would be taking notes. What I was doing all that time was reevaluating who I was, because all that information that these speakers and authors were sharing was about me. They were talking about the truth about myself. I was reevaluating who I was. I went from thinking that I didn't have anything going for me—that I was a useless character and I let my past dictate my future—to deciding that would have to change.

This process does take time. It doesn't have to take as long as it did with me, because it took years to learn what I'm explaining to you. Although I didn't realize then, I was changing my belief system by listening to those recordings over and over.

It's the repetition that alters what's going on inside of you. It's the repetition of hearing an idea that will change your belief system. When you keep listening to a recording telling you how good you are, and then backing that up with all kinds of evidence of why you're that good, and you listen to that over and over, you're going to start to believe it.

If you tell a person a lie often enough, they're going to believe it. Hitler proved that. He told people lies, but he was so persuasive that they believed him. Some still believe what he was doing was right. As ridiculous as this is, they believe it because they heard it so often.

When you keep hearing the same thing over and over again, you're going to start to believe it. We heard that if you don't go to school, you can't win. That's not true. Many people that have never seen in the inside of a school have built huge organizations. We were taught if you don't go to church, you're a sinner. That's not true either.

Why do we believe this? Because we heard it over and over again as children. It was programmed into our mind. As a result of hearing that repeatedly as little children, we develop that belief. We believe it from the moment we become aware of anything; it's part of our belief system.

I personally have come to the conclusion that we have to keep reevaluating our beliefs. Whenever you believe that you can't do something because of whatever condition or circumstance, it doesn't hold water. You've got to get to the point where you believe that there's something absolutely magnificent about you. There's something so incredible about us, and we can study it all our lives. As Earl Nightingale pointed out, our body is changing at the rate of about forty million cells per second. We're in a constant evolution of change.

Our belief system can change, and it is changing all the time. This change should involve upward growth, expansion, and fuller expression, because we're spiritual beings, and spirit always moves toward expansion and fuller expression. It's always for the greater good—not just sometimes: always. When we can understand that and lock into it, our lives are going to keep getting better and better.

Conscious versus Unconscious Belief

Sometimes as they're establishing a new belief system, people can lose confidence when they don't see the results they want right away. What should people do when their new vision of themselves isn't reflected in the results in the near term?

To understand this problem, you have to realize that you're dealing with two levels here: a conscious level and a subconscious level. You can believe something on a conscious level while not believing it on a subconscious level. Say you've read *Think and Grow Rich* and you believe that you can earn more money, but you're not earning it. Where's the problem? The belief is just in your intellect. It needs to be integrated into the subjective mind. Until it's properly planted in the subconscious, it's not going to manifest in results.

It's quite confusing to people when they know they believe something, but it's not showing up in their life.

It's a matter of praxis, which is the integration of belief with behavior. When you say, "I believe I can do something," and you're not doing it, it's because that belief has not been properly planted in the subconscious mind. Through repetition and proper visualization, it will be planted in the subconscious; then it starts manifesting as results.

Author George Leonard wrote a book called *Mastery*. He said that if you stay with something, you'll be on a plateau for a while. But you stay with the practice day in, day out, one day you'll suddenly hit a jump and find yourself at a new level. But you don't know when that jump's going to come. That's when you take a quantum leap.

When that mastery cuts in, there's an enormous change in results. It happens so fast, it's almost a shock. When my income went from $4,000 a year to $14,500 a month, it was a shock to my whole system. This happens when you master something.

This process probably takes a different length of time with every person. I think it depends on repetition—how often you study it and how deeply you study it. Repetition is the key.

People go to seminars, read books, and listen to recordings, but the results don't come, so they get very frustrated. They don't understand that all kinds of things happen that they cannot see. We're part of an unseen world; in fact the biggest part is the unseen. Nothing is created or destroyed, and the law of vibration decrees that everything vibrates on different frequencies. Every frequency is hooked up to the one above and the one below, so everything is connected. The unseen and the seen are connected. Spirit manifests through its polar opposite. Spirit is working within and through the physical body that you're living in.

The average individual knows nothing about that. Or they believe it intellectually, but it's not happening, and that causes frustration. Quite often, people will quit when they may only be, as Napoleon Hill said, three inches away from the riches.

In his book *You 2*, Price Pritchett wrote, "Absence of evidence is not evidence of absence." Then he added, "Think of an iceberg, where you see only the tip of what's really there, but just as real and out of sight are invisible sources ready to make a profound difference in what you can achieve."

We're dealing with something we don't understand, with something that's absolutely foreign to the minds of most people. The average individual knows very little about himself or herself. We learn nothing about ourselves in school. Even if you've studied psychology, you never really get into the essence of who you are. It's all left on an intellectual level; you never get into the spiritual essence of who we are, which is pretty sad.

When I first heard these ideas, I thought they were silly. But the man that explained it said, "My way's working, and yours is not. Why don't you try my way?" He was happy, healthy, and wealthy. I was unhappy, sick, and broke. He said, "Do exactly what I tell you until you find out I'm lying to you or I don't know what I'm talking about."

I thought that made sense, so I followed his advice. Immediately everything started to change. Of course, it started to change my belief system. Wernher von Braun, considered by many to be the father of the space program, said years of studying the spectacular mysteries of the cosmos led him to a firm belief in the existence of God. He said that the natural laws of this universe are so precise that we don't have any difficulty building spaceships, sending people to moon, and timing the landing within a fraction of a second. He said that these laws must have been set by somebody.

I like that. I've adopted that. The trick is understand the laws as best you can. Then you'll start to understand how things happen and how things can happen.

Overcome Distraction

As I've mentioned, when President Kennedy asked von Braun what it would take to build a rocket to go to the moon and come back safely, he said, "The will to do it."

The will is one of the higher faculties, and it gives us the ability to hold one idea on the screen of our mind to the exclusion of all outside distractions.

Unfortunately, we are distracted all the time. You see, hear, smell, taste, and touch, but those five senses merely connect you with the outside, material world. There's always activity going on out there, and it's always begging for your conscious attention. With the proper use of the will, you shut down those five senses and bring your mind into perfect harmony with the idea that you're focused on. That's what the great golfers do. That's what the great athletes do. That's what all the great salespeople do. That's what all the people who qualify as being great at anything do. They focus. They stick to their knitting. They don't wander all over the place.

As human beings, we share the spiritual aspect with the rest of creation; in fact, spirit is 100 percent present in all places at the same time. Spirit is omnipresent. Everything is spirit. There's nothing that is not spirit. It manifests in many forms, but it always manifest in its polar opposite, the physical form.

Although we share spirit with all that exists, what separates us from all the rest is that we are self-conscious. We are conscious of self. We have been given intellectual qualities that no other form of life, so far as we know, have been blessed with: perception, will, reason, imagination, memory, and intuition.

Each one of these faculties can be developed to a tremendous degree. They are reflected in the results; by their fruits you will know them. As I've said, most people know very little about these higher faculties. They only go by what they can see through their senses. If you're going to let the physical world control you, you're never going to have anything more than you've already got.

Everything in our material world is in the third dimension. You want to go beyond that into your higher faculties. If we're created in God's image, then all things are possible. We can do all things. We're not God, but we're an expression of God, and great work can be done. That's why Jesus said that even greater things are you capable of (John 14:12). You're dealing with an infinite power; there's no end to what you can do. It doesn't matter what it is or how good it is, it can still get better. I think *better* is such a beautiful word.

The emotions are in the driver's seat, they cause us to move, but the intellect dictates what goes into the emotional mind. The conscious mind reasons both inductively and deductively. The subconscious mind only reasons deductively; in other words, it can only accept; it cannot reject. Your conscious mind has an inductive reasoning capacity, which enables you to choose what's going into your subconscious mind. If you're not using that inductive reasoning faculty, if you've just lying dormant, whatever's going on around you is going right into your subconscious mind and will control your behavior.

How Advertising Works

That's how advertising works. It sets aside your inductive reasoning factor and opens up your subconscious mind, so you become totally deductive and do whatever you're told. You can set aside a person's inductive reasoning factor through fascination, agreement, or shock. That's how people become hypnotized. Hypnosis is nothing but suggestion. Advertising is a form of hypnosis. They fascinate you, shock you, set aside your inductive reasoning factor, and bang! A picture comes out and goes right into your subconscious mind. They don't do this once. They don't sell one commercial; they sell a flight of commercials. These are run over and over, and the message goes right into the subconscious mind. Eventually you find yourself doing what they want you to do, and you wonder why. It's because the idea has been planted in your mind.

Advertisers know that if they fire an idea at you often enough when you are in a certain mental state, you will act on that idea. They get you in a state of fascination. You're watching a movie: there's somebody sneaking up behind somebody. Your heart is pounding, you're on the edge of the chair, and all of a sudden, bang! There's a beautiful car in front of you. They don't do that once. They do that over and over. Then you wonder why you're wandering around the auto showroom.

The subconscious mind is where everything happens. It's what causes us to move into action. The conscious mind, though, can dictate what's going into the subconscious. You've got to think, but most people don't. You can tell that they're not thinking by watching them.

Response versus Reaction

Dr. Viktor Frankl wrote a marvelous book called *Man's Search for Meaning*. He was a Jewish psychiatrist in a concentration camp during the Second World War, and he wrote, "Regardless of the intellectual or physical abuse you're subjected to, no one can cause you to think something you do not want to think." He pointed out that in every situation, there is a space between the situation and your response to it. Now that space may be a millisecond, but in it you have the ability to choose whether you're going to react or respond.

If you merely react, you have given away your ability to choose to the circumstance or the person. You've given your power to whatever you're reacting to. If you say something that upsets me, then I've given my power to you; I've permitted you to upset me. I've quit thinking and run into my subconscious mind.

If I'm responding, I take a look and think, "I wonder why he said that. But it isn't true at all. I'm actually a very nice person. I don't have to accept that." Then you're not reacting, you're responding. That's what people have to learn to do. I've taught it to kids. It's changed their lives, because they were reacting to whatever was going on. I tell them, "When you're reacting, everything outside of you is in control of you; you're not in control of yourself at all."

In order to be able to respond instead of reacting, first of all, you have to become aware that you *are* reacting. You can react so fast. There's that expression: "She really knows how to press your buttons." For people to respond, they must think, and they've got to quit worrying about what other people think. If somebody says something offensive to you, you could react to that. They get angry, you get angry back; you yell at me, I'll yell at you. Nobody's going to win doing that.

When something like that happens, stop and ask yourself, why would they do that? Why would they say that? Our whole system is structured in such a way to make us to react.

We're acting on suggestion all the time. With all of this nonsense—yelling and fighting and riots—people are reacting to one another; they are not thinking. Then we try and quell them with more of the same thing. Fighting fire with fire won't work.

We've got to encourage people to stop and think, but we're not taught thinking in school. Thinking is a subject that can be taught, just like learning how to type or play a piano. You can be trained to use your higher faculties, your inductive reasoning powers. You can make up your mind that you're going to form the habit of responding rather than reacting to what goes on outside, and you can get good at it.

I'm not going to tell you that I never react, because I do. When I do, I become aware that I'm doing it, and I stop it. You can't win when you're reacting.

Problem Solving on Paper

I use a couple of techniques when I have a problem. First of all, I'll write it out on a piece of paper, as clearly as I can. After I've written it out, I'll go back and eliminate as many words as I can without losing the idea. I want it so that if I were to give you the paper and you were to read it, you would see the problem as I see it.

When I've set out the problem that way, then I'll go and sit at a different place at the table. In my home, I'll put it on my dining room table. If I'm in my office, I'll put it in the center of my desk. Then I'll sit at another place, and I'll ask, "How would Earl Nightingale look at this?" I'll mentally try and get into Earl's energy. How would he perceive this? How would he look at this?

After I've played with the question like that, I may sit at another place and ask, "How would Napoleon Hill look at this?" I may then sit somewhere else and ask, "How would Andrew Carnegie look at this?" I'll pick a half a dozen people—maybe Edison or Henry Ford—and mentally get into their energy. Pretty soon I'm looking at it in a totally different way.

I've already quoted my late friend Wayne Dyer: "When you change the way you look at something, what you look at will change." That's shifting your perception of the situation. Now that's one thing to do, and it works like a charm.

Next, you want to work from the high to the low. Coming from high to low means going from spirit down to the intellect to the physical realm. Always work from spirit to the intellectual and physical. If you're working with electricity, you must work from a higher to a lower potential. If you try to go contrary to that law, you're not going to get any use out of electricity.

The spirit is on the thought level. You're coming from the inside out, not from the outside in. You don't look at present results and let them control you, as most people do. They go from the outside in, and up from the bottom. They focus on the problem, then they pray to an unseen God in a cloud somewhere to fix it.

We're spiritual beings, so we can go into our spiritual self, into the thought world. Thought is omnipresent; so is spirit. When he was voyaging to the moon, Captain Edgar Mitchell was doing thought transference exercises, which were later written up in a psychology magazine.

Your thoughts are omnipresent. When you're thinking, you're working with an enormous power. Thought is the most potent energy there is: it makes the laser beam look small. You start from the thought to the idea to the thing. You don't work from the outside in: work from the inside out. I've been doing this for a long time. It works like a charm. When you're working in harmony with the law, everything flows beautifully. When you're not, it's not beautiful. It's pretty rough.

Chapter Six

The Paradigm for Power Performance

*L*et me now talk about ways to use this powerful mind of ours so as to form a paradigm for power performance.

One of the primary qualities is a great attitude. As I've said, my mentor Earl Nightingale called *attitude* the magic word. How does a person use the mind to develop a great attitude? What habits can you practice on a daily basis to reinforce it?

I study continually. I have books on my desk: I have *You 2* by Price Pritchett; *Ask!* by Mark Victor Hansen and his wife Crystal; *You Too Can Be Prosperous* by Robert Russell; *The Power of Awareness* by Neville; and *Think and Grow Rich* by Napoleon Hill. I've always got books on my desk.

I have Thomas Troward's books in my book holder. If you're not into Troward's material, you may want to take a look at it. Earl Nightingale was reading Troward's *Edinburgh Lectures on Mental Science* when I visited him in 1968. I asked Earl, "Should I read this?" He just looked at me and said, "Yes." It probably took me until 1970 to understand what I was reading; I'd read a page, but I didn't know what I had read. Anyway, it's phenomenal information.

I keep my attitude right by studying constantly. The only way to improve is through study. There is no other way. You're trying to gain a greater understanding of who you are and your relationship with everything in the universe.

Also, I'm continually attempting to improve what we're doing in our company. I'm always wanting to raise our sales; I want to sell more. I'm working with the sales department about ideas in selling. I am always creating new programs. Right now I'm creating a master class on *You Were Born Rich*, which I wrote in 1984. I started studying in 1961, so I'd been studying for twenty-three years before I wrote it. Its subjects are all great: "Me and Money"; "Let Go, Let God"; "The Law of Vibration." It's been over thirty-six years since I wrote that book, but I can use the same subjects, because I understand them much better and can go much deeper.

Furthermore, you've got to have goals. You've got to be raising the bar for yourself all the time, being aware that your attitude is going to determine your success or failure. Then you're going to keep going in the right direction.

Decision, Visualization, Discipline

Here are some basic, simple rules: if you follow them, you win; if you violate them, you lose. There are three things that a person absolutely must lock into if they really want to set a higher goal and go after it. The first is *decision*. The second is understanding *visualization*, and the third is *discipline*. That's how I keep my attitude right and keep things moving in the right direction for myself and the company.

I've mentioned Neville more than once, and like many other people in the personal development industry, I've been inspired by him and his works. One things that changed my attitude from negativity to positivity is repeating a question of his right before I go to bed: now that my dream is fulfilled, how do I feel?

I work on different questions, different dreams, all the time, and the feeling is very important. It's not how you think about it; it's how you feel. We don't become what we think, but we do become what we feel, because thinking is in the conscious mind, feeling is in the subconscious: that's the universal side of our personality. It involves visualization; you have to see it fulfilled.

You've got to work *from* the end, not *to* it. When you've done that right, you're on the right track; it's only a matter of time until your goal manifests in form, because you've already accomplished it in your intellect and your emotional mind. No one, of course, knows what the gestation period for an idea is. That's where faith comes in.

I want to touch on some other aspects of a power performance paradigm. The first idea is, take responsibility for how you feel and act. Energy is flowing through us, and it's up to us to direct it in any way we want.

We could think of it this way: We are spiritual beings. We don't have a soul; we *are* soul. Spirit awaits direction from the soul. That's why we're told, "Ask, and you'll be given." You have to build the image of where you want to go. Spirit is always flowing to and through us, and we've got to direct it. The soul is forever directing the energy that flows to and through it.

It's up to us. God doesn't decide where we're going; we make those decisions. God does the work, but we decide; God does all the work through us. God, who is in every cell of our being, operates in a lawful, orderly manner. It takes our image and turns it over, and that's when it starts moving into form.

The second principle is, decide what you want, and act as if you have it. What you want is already here, if not in one state, then in another. Most people don't understand that. They don't understand that nothing is created or destroyed; everything is already here. That's why Wernher von Braun told President Kennedy that all was required to land a man on the moon was the will to do it. The ways and means to accomplish our goals are already here. We just have to get in touch with them. When you make a decision, the only prerequisite is, do you want it?

Operating on Frequencies

You're operating on frequencies. Visualize a series of lines in front of you, like on a lined pad. Each line represents a level of vibration, or a frequency. If you put an R on a line towards the bottom of the pad and say, "That R represents results," that's where you are right now. Now go way up on the pad, towards the top, and over on the right-hand side, put a star. It's on a higher line, on a higher frequency. That's what you want. You've got to move yourself and your consciousness onto that line, onto that frequency, or you're never going to reach your goal. You've got to act like the person you want to become. You've got to get on that frequency and live there.

That's the only way your desired result is going to come to you. Most people just dream about their goals; they never reach them. You've got to act like the person you want to become. You've got to *be* it. That's why Goethe, the German philosopher, said, "Before you can do something, you first must *be* something."

Your Power Life Script

One technique I've discussed in my seminars is writing out a power life script in the present tense and recording it in your own voice. You write out how you want to live, everything you want, in as much detail as you can. It's always in the present tense, and you're always being thankful for it: "I am so happy and grateful now that . . ." You've got to take your mind to that place, and you've got to live there, which is not an easy thing to do. You describe what you're thinking, what you're doing, how you're living; that's your life script.

Your friends at work, your next-door neighbor, your brother-in-law are going to say, "Who do you think you are?" We don't like that, so we don't go there; we've got to get past what they think. If you don't see yourself already there, talk like it, walk like it, and act like it, you're never going to be there.

That's why the imagination is a magnificent tool. Imagination isn't something that kids play with; it's something that all wise people use to create the good—on the level of mind, to start off with. We take ourselves to where we want to be and see ourselves already there. We walk like we're there, we talk like we're there, and we act like we're there, because in our mind, we *are* there.

That's what prayer is. Prayer is the movement that takes place between spirit and form, with and through us. All prayers are answered. Most people think praying is getting on your knees and talking. That's not praying; that's making noise on your knees. A minister once told me, "Praying is what most people do between prayers." If you think about that, you'll realize how accurate he was. Prayer is when you mentally go into what you desire in spirit; you get into the spirit of it. Then you let it go through to your whole being; that's when it begins to move into form. Now it's only a matter of time until your dream manifests in physical form, and other people will be able to see what you've been seeing for quite a while.

Earl Nightingale said, "This great dream, the surging dynamic thing invisible to all the world, except to the person who holds it, is responsible for every great advance of mankind." That's one of my favorite quotes.

Another valuable aspect of writing and recording a power life script is that many of us are used to having the chatter and self-talk of fear in our minds. It's trying to pull us back into the old paradigm, rehearsing our fears inside our heads and hearing this as our voice. If you write out this present-tense power life script in your own voice and you listen to yourself speak this reality over and over again, it rescripts that inner voice toward what you want. It's powerful, because you trust your own voice. It's got to get into your subconscious mind.

That's what all great actors do. If you really want to get into this concept, get Stella Adler's book *The Art of Acting*. Stella Adler was a great method acting teacher. Marlon Brando was her student and was the first student of method acting to hit superstardom. He wrote the foreword to that book. Actually, Stella Adler never wrote a book. She had lessons, and when she passed away, a man named Howard Kissel took them and put them in a book, *The Art of Acting*. It's magnificent.

As William James said, "Act like the person you want to become." Yul Brynner, I understand, played the role of the king of Siam in *The King and I* onstage three thousand times. Every time, it was as if were doing it for the first time. He understood how to get into the part.

When George C. Scott was shooting the movie *Patton*, he became so much like General Patton that he scared some of Patton's friends who were on the set. George C. Scott was a great actor. All the great actors live their parts. That's what we've got to do. We've got to write the script and live the part. That's how it moves into form.

Your Accountability Partner

Another important idea in the paradigm for power performance is getting an accountability partner. We say we're going to do things, and when we say that, we probably believe it. But life frequently gets in the road, and we don't. Even when people say they're committed to a course of action, they still don't carry it out.

When you make an irrevocable commitment, and you have an accountability partner, you're accountable to that person. Pick an accountability partner whom you respect and whom you want to respect you. You say, "This I will do," and they hold you accountable for that. You don't want to let them down. You don't want to look bad in their eyes. The odds of you doing it have increased substantially.

I've already discussed the accountability methods used by Sandy Gallagher and me. Every morning I write out my sentences three times, then I record them, and then I send them in a text. I don't want her to think that I'm not doing that, because I want her to respect me, and I know she wants me to respect her. We use this approach with various projects we're involved in; we're just phenomenal partners.

Sandy is very good at what I'm not good at, and I'm very good at what she's not good at. Recently we were talking about a particular person in our company, and I said, "That person's not aware of what they're not good at, and that's causing them a problem."

You've got to be aware of what you're not good at. It's OK not to be good at it. As I've pointed out, you don't have to be good at everything. There are some things I know I'm never going to be good at; I don't even want to try. I have somebody else doing those things. Instead, I take what I do and work to get better at it every day. Get better what you're good at, manage what you're not good at, and be accountable to someone. Make sure that when you say you're going to do something, it's going to get done.

Feel the Vision

The next point is to hold the vision and feel it naturally. Through regular conditioning of your thoughts and scripts about your goals, what once feels unnatural eventually feels natural.

You could relate this to driving a car. When I first started, I didn't think I'd ever learn how to drive. My mother was teaching me; she yelled at me, and I yelled back. She'd say, "Don't you yell at me; I'm your mother!" At the same time I was trying to figure how to change gears, let the clutch out, and step on the brake at the right time. It felt very uncomfortable and scary, but later you're not even thinking about driving: you're doing it all on a subconscious level. By repeatedly doing the thing you're uncomfortable with, you'll eventually start feeling comfortable with it.

Say there's an X idea in your subconscious mind, and a Y idea in your conscious mind. X is the programming, the paradigm. The Y idea is the new idea—say, quit your job and start your own business. You try to get emotionally involved with the Y idea, but the X is quickly going to kick it out. It'll cause you to feel very uncomfortable with the thought of quitting your job and starting your own business. Mortgage your business, mortgage your house, take all your savings—a scary idea. But if you keep playing with that Y idea and getting emotionally involved with it, pretty soon the Y idea becomes an X idea, and you're comfortable with it.

That's what we must do. We must keep getting emotionally involved in the idea that causes discomfort, and pretty soon it will become quite comfortable. That's when we've turned it into part of the paradigm.

Comfort is not a good place to be. If you're really comfortable with everything in your life, you're stuck, you're going sideways; you're not growing at all. You've got to be doing something that causes a respectable amount of discomfort and keep doing it until you're comfortable with it. When you are, then set another target that causes discomfort. That discomfort indicates that you're growing; you're going where you've never been.

Set a New Standard

You also need to set a new standard. This is part of the self-esteem concept. I always attempt to emulate people that I really admire. I want to understand this material as well as Earl Nightingale understood it. I want to understand it as well as Thomas Troward understood it, as well as Neville understood it. I pick people who are giants in this industry, and I attempt to emulate them.

I don't want to copy these people. In his essay "Self-Reliance," Emerson said something brilliant: "There is a time in every man's education when he arrives at the conviction that envy is ignorance; imitation is suicide; that he must take himself, for better, for worse, as his portion."

To envy another person is to look at them and say, "I'm not aware that I have the power in me that they've got in them. They use that power to achieve the results they're getting. I don't know that I've got that, so I will envy them. I wish I had their results; I wish I was doing what they were doing." That's what envy is: ignorance. And "imitation is suicide." There's no way you can be like anyone else.

There's a beautiful poem by James T. Moore that I put it in the *Born Rich* book:

One and Only You
Every single blade of grass,
And every flake of snow—
Is just a wee bit different . . .
There's no two alike, you know.
From something small, like grains of sand,
To each gigantic star
All were made with THIS in mind:
To be just what they are!
How foolish then, to imitate—
How useless to pretend!
Since each of us comes from a MIND
Whose ideas never end.
There'll only be just ONE of ME
To show what I can do—
And you should likewise feel very proud,
There's only ONE of YOU.
That is where it all starts
With you, a wonderful
unlimited human being.

Self-Discipline

The next point is to develop self-discipline. It's not that you're not disciplined; it's that you've never put a high enough priority on becoming disciplined. Give yourself a command to do what you're going to say.

I think everybody's disciplined. Some people are disciplined regarding the wrong things; they do it regardless. Addicts are disciplined. They turned their desire into addiction. I see discipline as the ability to give ourself a command and then follow it: "This I will do." If I just did that, I'd get much better results.

Discipline is a command you give to yourself that's going to improve everything that you do. I recently sent a text to a lady. She had started listening to a recording that I had made for her; she used it for a while and stopped, then started to use it again. I found out about it, so I sent her a text saying, "Congratulations! I understand you're using the recording again. The discipline that you will develop listening to this every day for the next thirty or sixty days is going to impact all other areas of your life."

Use Autosuggestion

Another valuable technique is to use autosuggestion in your daily practice. Autosuggestion is a suggestion from yourself to yourself. It's an idea that you originate in the conscious mind and turn over to the subconscious mind. We're involved in autosuggestion all the time: every thought we think and get emotionally involved with is a suggestion.

It's like self-hypnosis. When somebody else is giving you a hypnotic suggestion, it's coming from somewhere else. You want to keep repeating the same concept to yourself over and over.

Earl Nightingale once made a recording called *That's Good*, describing a situation with his friend W. Clement Stone. W. Clement Stone started with nothing. By the end of his life, he was one of the wealthiest men in the world. Stone had formed the habit of saying, "That's good." It didn't matter what happened; he'd say, "That's good." If you look for good in everything, you will find good in everything, because there is good in everything.

My dear friend Michael Beckwith once shared an idea that I love. He said when anything happens, there's a three-step approach to it:

1. Look at it and say, "It is what it is"; accept it. It's either going to control you, or you're going to control it. (There's your react-respond dichotomy again.)

2. Harvest the good. There's good in everything. The more you look for, the more you'll find.

3. Forgive all the rest. Forgive, let it go, completely abandon it.

Eliminate Procrastination

The next principle is, eliminate procrastination and accelerate towards your goals. I think there's only one way to handle this. Everything has an opposite. The opposite to procrastination is decision. When people come to me and they tell me they've got a problem with procrastination, I tell them to find someone and have the two of you make a commitment that every day for sixty days that you will read the chapter on decision in *Think and Grow Rich*. It's the longest chapter in the book, and it's incredible.

When you're reading this chapter, the two of you don't have to be in the same city or the same place. You can phone each other. One of you starts reading, reads a few lines, and says, "Pass." The other persons picks it up there, starts reading a few lines, and says, "Pass." Both of you have to be reading while the other person reads, or you won't know where to pick up. If you do that for sixty days, you will eliminate procrastination, which is simply a matter of not making a decision.

The Lessons of Gratitude in Freedom

*G*ratitude is a magnificent concept. It's funny that it should be chapter seven of this book, because on the first page of chapter seven in *The Science of Getting Rich*, Wallace Wattles points out that "the entire process of mental adjustment and atonement can be summed up in one word, gratitude."

A Writing Exercise

Whenever you're disturbed, whenever things are bothering you, sit down somewhere where it's quiet. Take a pen and a pad and ask, "What do I have to be grateful for?" Don't just treat this as an intellectual exercise, where you jot some stuff down. What are you grateful for? Write it all down.

Sandy Gallagher and I were doing a seminar in Phoenix. I was leaving town, because I'd finishing the part I was doing. Sandy said she had a couple of personal challenges; could I sit down and talk to her about them?

I said, "Sure. Come on; we'll go across the road," where there was an old coffee shop.

In the coffee shop I took a napkin out of a holder. And I said, "As a first step, I want you to write down ten things you're grateful for. Then think of three people that are bothering you, and send them love. Number three: totally relax for five minutes, meditate, and ask for good energy for the rest of the day."

I phoned Gina, who's worked with me for over thirty years now—she is an incredible assistant—and said, "Gina, could you make up a pad and get it printed over at Kinko's?" Within an hour, she came back. The pad had "Gratitude" at the top of it, "Sandy Gallagher," at the bottom and the numbers one through ten down the side for her to write down ten things to be grateful for. Then it said, "Send love to three people that bother you." The next one: "Relax for five minutes, and ask for guidance for the day.

Gina got three pads for her. Sandy was going to Hawaii the next day with her mother and her sister, so she took a pad for each of them. The first morning, her mother and sister thought she was crazy. Then they started doing this practice to amuse her and fell in love with the idea. They started doing it every morning. They're probably still doing it.

Gratitude is the attitude that hooks you up to your source of supply. Send love to people that bother you when you would probably like them to be in a car accident. After all, if somebody has hurt me and I'm sending bad thoughts to them, who's in the bad vibration? It's got to come to and through me. The trick is to control the flow. Energy flows to and through you. You've got to send love to those people that are bothering you: that puts you in a loving vibration. The benefit for you is enormous. Love everybody.

Then totally relax, and ask for guidance for the day. I do that every morning.

Some of the stories that Sandy tells about that experience, from both business and personal perspectives, are mind-boggling. It changed her life. In one case, she was having a tough time with some people: it was going to go to court. She imagined that this matter would all work out perfectly, and she gave thanks for and sent to love to these people. Within less than a week, that problem, which she'd been struggling with for a couple of months, was solved.

This is one of the most beneficial ideas you'll ever get. Make a commitment to do this gratitude exercise before you go to bed. The feeling of gratitude is an incredible vibration, and it hooks you up to your source of supply.

Put Yourself on a Frequency of Love

When you put yourself onto a frequency of love, love is all you can attract. You can only attract that which resonates with you. It's all induction resonance. You're dealing with electronics: your body is an electronic instrument, it's a mass of molecules on a very high speed of vibration.

Doing this practice puts you onto an incredible vibration, and you start to attract good things into your life. Things happen that you never knew would happen. Your perception is going to shift, and you won't have bad feelings about anyone. You stop reacting. When you start asking for guidance, you'd be amazed how fast and how beautiful it is when it comes—and it will come all the time. You may stop to do this anytime through the day: if you're a little troubled, just stop, be quiet, and ask for guidance. It will always come. Ask, and you'll receive.

In addition, you can keep a gratitude journal. A gratitude journal is invaluable. I think the morning is a great time to set up an attitude of gratitude. Set up the habit of writing down ten things you're grateful for, sending love to anybody that's bothering you, and asking for guidance for the day.

You may want to use this practice through the day. If you a problem surfaces, journal it. Don't use this gratitude journal for ordinary notes; use it for what it's designed for. When you're a little troubled, you feel overwhelmed, or you feel you're certain to react to what's going on in the day, get the gratitude journal out.

As Wallace Wattles said, gratitude is "the entire process of mental adjustment." If you're having a problem, you need a mental adjustment, because all problems originate in your mind. A mentor once told me, "You're the only problem you will ever have, Bob, and you're the only solution." He was right. You are the only problem you will ever have, and you are the only solution. When you understand that, you'll start to see the value in sitting down and becoming grateful every day whenever you're having a bit of a problem. It's such a phenomenal attitude, and it changes your life.

Just Walk Away

Another powerful idea for changing your paradigm has to do with freedom. Many times, when people look at changing something in their lives, it's to become more free. In our seminars, my partner, Sandy Gallagher, sometimes says, "Respect yourself enough to walk away from anything that no longer serves you, helps you to grow, or makes you happy."

We're the only ones that can set ourselves free. As Bill Gove said, "If I want to be free, I've got to be me. Not the me I think you think I should be, not the me I think my wife thinks I should be; not the me I think my kids think I should be. If want to be free, I've got to be me. I've got to know who *me* is."

It goes back to studying ourselves: understanding what thinking is actually about, how our mind functions, how the conscious works versus the subconscious, the role that our senses play versus our higher faculties. When we really start to understand all this, I think we enjoy a greater degree of freedom.

The freedom that I am enjoying today is far removed from where I was when I first picked up *Think and Grow Rich* in 1961. I was twenty-six. I'd never read a book in my life, and I looked at this book and thought it was so thick. Now I've got marvelous libraries in my house and studio. I love books. I've come to love to read, and I think the more you read, the freer you'll become.

Freedom comes from understanding ourselves and our relationship with our God. The lack of understanding creates a prison for oneself. Some people live in prisons of their own making. In his play *The Secret of Freedom*, Archibald MacLeish has a character stand up and say, "The only thing about a man that is a man is his mind. Everything else you'll find in a pig or a horse." The more we study, the freer we become. The more aware we become, the freer we become.

Financial Freedom

I think everybody should have a goal of being financially free. You'll be amazed how much free time you have when you never have to think about money. If you have to think about how you're going to pay the mortgage, you're not free; you're in a prison of your own making, because anyone can create financial freedom in a relatively short period of time. To do that, they have to create a new paradigm. They should go to somebody who knows how to create financial freedom and then exactly do what that person tells them. I formed that habit a long time ago, and it works very well. That is the only way that you'll ever experience freedom.

Here's a quote that Sandy and I use in our seminars: "Peel off the mask of illusion, unshackle the chains of expectation, release the ingrained patterns learned, give up the stories of the past, let go of the fear. It's never too late to be who you really are."

When they're first exposed to these ideas, people might hear a little voice that says, "But, Bob, I have others that depend on me—my spouse, my kids, my employees, and they expect things from me. How can I simply unshackle those chains? How can I release the ingrained patterns that were impressed upon me for twenty years? I had an abusive upbringing. For years, my teachers told me that I wasn't smart and would never amount to anything. How can I release all that?"

I don't think this process takes place overnight. It's more of a long-term objective that all people could work toward. I feel I've done what that quote above says, although it's not easy. That's what changing a paradigm is all about. We've got so many false beliefs that we allow to chain us down.

In a great book, *The Mystic Path to Cosmic Power*, Vernon Howard said, "You cannot escape from a prison if you don't know you're in one." Most people are in a prison of their own making, but they don't know they are. If a person analyzes that quote, they'll realize there's a certain amount in their life that's false and doesn't hold any semblance of truth. We've got to get away from that.

Many people feel responsible for others, but actually we are not responsible for anyone else. We're responsible for our children until they reach a certain age; then we're responsible *to* them but not *for* them. There's a big difference between being responsible *to* and being responsible *for*. Many parents are having a terrible time because they feel responsible for their kids, although the kids are thirty-five or forty. The parents are not responsible for them at all. They were at one time, but that time passed quite a while ago.

In the end, freedom is a very personal matter. We shouldn't try to impose our own thoughts on other people. In Earl Nightingale's program, he says, "I'm not going to try and tell you how to live your life." Rather he gives you great suggestions, and if you follow them, you will live a very good life. By following them to the best of my ability for almost all of my adult life, I enjoy a degree of freedom today that I didn't think was possible when I started studying. And it keeps getting better.

We're born free, but then we're not. We're born with all the tools to create the freedom, but we've also inherited many false beliefs and paradigms. Somebody else originated them many, many moons ago. Now it's up to us to recognize what beliefs we are operating with that are false and get rid of them. That's really the trick of life. I have spent many years, and I will spend the rest of my life, doing that.

Chapter Eight

The Benefits of Changing Your Paradigm

*I*n this chapter, I want to look at the effects that you'll see in your life from changing your paradigm.

Changing Your Perception

The first thing is perception. You cause your paradigm change by shifting your perception. Take the ability to earn money. Today, without any difficulty, I can earn more money in an hour than I used to earn in an entire year when I first picked up *Think and Grow Rich*. I had the ability to do that then, I had all the talent within, but I wasn't aware of it. My perception of life kept me stuck where I was. I thought this was normal for me. It wasn't normal at all, but I accepted it, because I really didn't think I could change it.

I did change my belief system, but a shift in perception precedes the change in belief. You can close your eyes and change your perception. Perception is a mental faculty that enables you to change how you see things. It enables you to become aware of the power and potential that you have but weren't even aware of.

Perception is a mental tool. It is to the mind what hearing or sight is to the body. Our physical senses enable us to communicate with the material world. Our higher faculties enable us to communicate with the unseen world, with the world we have never even seen, that we're not even aware of.

Our creative faculties enable us to create the kind of world we want. The first thing you have to do is see it in your mind. You've got to shift how you look at things. When you change your perception of yourself and what you're capable of doing, the world starts to spin totally differently for you.

Mastering Time

Another area of life that will change as a result of shifting your paradigm is your use of time. Everybody gets exactly the same amount of time, so it's what we do with our time that makes a difference. From the perspective of service, I accomplish more now in a day than I would have done in a year prior to studying any of this.

Let's suppose a salesperson makes one extra call a day. When they're finished, they say, "I'll make one more call," and they do that five times a week. Let's suppose that this isn't a very good salesperson, who closes one out of five sales presentations. They would be making fifty sales a year that they wouldn't otherwise have made. Let's suppose they're earning $100 a sale: that's $5,000 a year extra.

Earl Nightingale got more done in a short period of time than anybody I've known. I never saw the man hurry anywhere. I watched him for five years of working with him. He accomplished more in a short period of time than anyone else I've ever known.

One day I went on a speaking engagement with Earl in downtown Chicago. I'd never had a chance to be with him alone, so I jumped at the chance. When we were having breakfast prior to the engagement, I asked him, "Earl, how did you learn to master time management?"

He looked at me and said, "What the hell are you talking about? I've never mastered time management; nobody does. Time can't be managed. I merely manage activities." He pulled a card out of his pocket and said, "I merely write down at night what I'm going to do the next day. The next day I wake up, and I do those things. It's all decided."

Once I developed a seminar called "A Sense of Urgency." I see a sense of urgency in a person who's able to get a lot done in a short period of time in a calm, confident manner. If a person doesn't have a sense of urgency and they've got a lot to do, they probably cause confusion and panic with everybody they come in contact with. With a sense of urgency, you get a lot done in a short time, in a calm, confident manner.

A lot of what we're doing, we don't have to do at all, so you can save a lot of time there. Some of the things we think have to get done will get done through neglect. They don't have to be done at all.

You also have to delegate. Once my wife was overwhelmed, with a ton of work on her desk. She asked, "Will you help me?"

"OK," I said, "but you've got to do what I tell you."

"I will," she said.

She had all kinds of things piled on the desk. I picked up one at a time and said, "What's this? Does this have to be done?"

"Yes," she said.

"Well, then, do you have to do it?"

"I really don't." She had an assistant named Helen.

In the end my wife didn't have too much to do, although now Helen did. She asked, "How's she going to do that?"

"That's Helen's problem. It's not yours." I said, "If Helen can't get it all done, she'll have to hire an assistant, but she has to hire the assistant, not you. If you hire the assistant, the assistant will be working for you, not for Helen."

My wife learned a lot that day. She became much more productive, because she learned that many of the things she was doing, she didn't have to do at all.

Utilize Creativity

The third area of life influenced by our paradigm is creativity. I can use myself as a pretty good example. When I finished the eighth grade, My teacher asked, "Bob, where are you going to go to high school?"

"I'm going to Malvern Collegiate."

"Oh, Bob, don't go there. You'll never do well in business. Go to Danforth Tech and get a trade."

What did I know? My teacher was like God, so I went to Danforth Tech. I was only there for a month. I shoved my thumb into a band saw and cut the end of it off. They sewed it back on. Years and years later, it still hurts when it gets cold.

I'm very creative. I create all kinds of wonderful programs, and I've written a few books. I'm a very right-brained person. Right-brained people are very creative.

My teacher didn't know that; neither did the people who were helping raise me.

Some people seem to be more adept at creativity than others, but no one's more creative than anyone else. We are all creative; it's just that some utilize their creative abilities more. We're all truly expressions of God. Our higher faculties are the creative faculties of perception, will, reason, imagination, and memory. We've got to learn what they're for and how to utilize them; then we become very creative. There's a better way to do every-thing, and we can find it if we're looking for it.

An associate of mine once said she had never met another person like me. She said, "You've recreated your-self more often than Madonna." I'm always recreating myself, but I see it as finding a better way to help people understand what they've got going for them.

There's a clear, unadulterated power that flows to and through us. It can be photographed leaving your body. Semyon Kirlian, the Russian photographer, perfected a technique for doing that way back in 1934. When that power flows into our consciousness, it has no form. We give it form. That's where the creation starts. In truth, nothing is created or destroyed, so we're taking one form of energy and causing it to move into a different form of energy, which would have never happened if we hadn't been there and moved it. We play a very big role in life.

Productivity and Effectiveness

Productivity and effectiveness are the fourth major area of life that's influenced by our paradigm. Productivity and effectiveness are like a chicken and an egg: one affects the other. As we become more effective at what we do, we automatically become more productive.

We can become much more productive. We've got to look for better ways of doing what we're doing. To me, 1980 seems like a relatively short period of time ago. The fax was just coming into play then. Now it seems so antiquated. I can take a picture on my phone and hit "send," and you've got it immediately. This is all a form of productivity: utilizing our creative faculties in a more effective manner. It's figuring out how to do what we're doing better than we were doing it—faster, with less cost and less effort.

I'm of the opinion that if you're struggling, you're doing it wrong. If you're working in harmony with the law, it's going to be a free flow. We have the mental faculties to cause these creative energies to flow into any state or any form that we want. We've got awesome powers locked up within us that we're really not familiar with. Some people are not aware of them at all.

Regardless of how much you're struggling right now or how difficult things are, you can become much more effective. When you do, you're going to be rewarded for it.

Logic versus Illogic

The fifth area to be affected by a paradigm change is our use of logic. Logic is like precedent: it's how it's always been done; it's the limit to what we do. If somebody says, "That's not logical," that will probably inspire me to go and do it.

I'm not interested in whether something is logical or illogical. The question is, do you want it? Do you want to do it? Do you want it to happen? Then forget logic; just go do it. There is a story that Thomas Edison was sent home from the third grade with a note in a sealed envelope telling his mother, "Please do not send him back to school. He just didn't have what it took to do what they were doing." His mother put the note back in the envelope and told him that he wouldn't be going back to school because he already knew more than what they were teaching. She would start teaching him at home.

We've got to realize a better way to do everything. We don't want to let anything slow us down. If we get a picture of it in our mind, we can do it. If you can see it in your head, you can hold it in your hand. Then you've got to massage it, work with it, if you want it to turn into form. Just seeing it in your mind isn't good enough, although it's an indication that you can do it.

Change Your Money Paradigm

The sixth major area of life affected by a paradigm change has to do with money. Your paradigm can set boundaries around how much money you can earn, and by changing your paradigm, you can radically change those boundaries. Your paradigm isn't going to stop you from earning less, but it is going to stop you from earning more.

Money is earned not by work, but by providing a service. The more creative you are, the more service you can render. I earn money twenty-four hours a day, even though I'm sleeping through a good part of it, and anybody can. We teach people how to do that. We teach people to set up multiple sources of income.

There's no end to what you can earn, although people think there is. One of the first things I ask a client when I start working with him is, what's the most you've ever earned in a year? I don't really care what the answer is, but it will tell me where your paradigm is set. Money is a good yardstick for paradigms, because money can be measured right to the penny. Health cannot. You can go to a doctor and the doctor will say you're in perfect health, then you could walk out and drop dead. That's happened many times.

In my seminars, I teach people how to earn money. A publishing company said that I was America's greatest prosperity teacher, because I'm really focused on that. I've focused on it because I think it has such an impact in people's lives. You can do so much good with money that you cannot do if you don't have it.

Money is not going to make you a better person, but it will make you more of what you already are. If you're not a nice person, you're going to become despicable. If you are a nice person, you will become much nicer. Money's a magnifier. There's no limit to what you can earn, but to earn it, you have to provide service. That doesn't mean you have to work, but you have to provide service.

How many millions of dollars does the singer Taylor Swift earn in a year? And she doesn't really work that hard, although she probably has spells where she gives a lot of energy to her music. Every time one of her recordings is played, she earns some money, and of course, millions of people are listening to her recordings. She's entertaining them, she deserves to be rewarded for that, and she is.

Money is a reward we receive for service rendered. As I've already emphasized, the amount of money you earn is in direct ratio to the need for what you do, your ability to do it, and the difficulty there is in replacing you.

Years ago, at a place where I worked, I went up and asked the president what I had to do to earn more money.

"Do you want a raise?" he asked.

"No. I don't want a raise," I said. "I just want to know what I have to do to earn more money."

"How much do you want to earn?"

I think was back in the 1970s. I said, "I don't know—$100,000."

"You couldn't earn $100,000."

"Why not?"

"I said you couldn't. That's all there is to it." I knew that my ten years there was shortly going to be coming to an end, because somebody else was deciding how much I could earn.

Never let anybody decide what you're going to earn. That's something you've got to decide. If you're letting somebody else decide, and you're not happy with it, you know what you have to do: you have to get out of there and go out on your own.

Entrepreneurship is incredible. I personally believe that network marketing is one of the greatest ideas that ever come down the road. I'm not in network marketing, I'm much too mature to go and work in another field, but it's a place where you automatically set up multiple sources of income. Wealthy people historically have had multiple sources of income.

The ability to earn money is definitely a matter of your paradigm. If I'm working with people, that's one of the first things I change. I'm always attempting to get our salespeople to set larger income earning goals, and they do. Some people in our company earn over $1 million a year. One guy might go up to around $4 million or $5 million this year.

There's no limit to what we can earn, and we've got to understand that. We've got to understand the law governing the earning of money, and then we've got to get busy doing it. As I've mentioned, we started a company, or rather a division of our company: MSI Connect. MSI stands for *multiple sources of income*. You connect with other people that are setting up multiple sources of income. Thousands of people all over the world belong to MSI Connect and are working together and helping one another. It's a great way to earn money. They can go in and sell something and somebody else can come and buy it. We've got a big marketplace. We deal with a lot of people.

Selling is the highest-paid profession in the world. A commission salesperson is the highest paid person in the world. No one can earn the amount of money a salesperson can earn. Nobody can come close.

We have to realize that everything we could ever want is already here. We've got to get in harmony with it. When we think of a good that we would like to have that we haven't got, we're not in harmony with it. The question is, how do I get in harmony with it? How do I raise my own level of conscious awareness? Study is the only way. I can't do it for you, and you can't do it for me. I couldn't do it for my children, and you can't do it for yours. You can't do it for your wife, and your wife can't do it for you.

We're the only ones that can do it for ourselves, but we've got to get involved, understanding that all things are possible. That is not just some nice religious statement. That is a fact. I believe I'm an excellent example of that; if I can win, anybody can. The odds of it happening were ridiculously remote, but it happened, for a good reason: I read good books, I listened to good recordings, I was tutored by excellent people. I chose my mentors. I don't mix with anyone who isn't working on goals, who isn't going somewhere in their life. I don't want to hang around people who are complaining. I subscribe to Earl Nightingale's principle: don't talk about your health unless you're talking to a doctor. If someone starts complaining about their health to me, I tell them I'm not a doctor. It's something we can work at and we can do it, we can do it well.

Get a good teacher. Good teachers are worth their weight in gold. If I'm mentoring a person, it will cost them a lot of money, but they quickly find out that I'm worth a lot of money. I teach them how to become worth a lot of money.

Everyone is worth a lot. It's just that everyone doesn't believe it. When we do, everything starts changing, regardless of where a person's at. No matter how much they may be struggling, they can change it. They have to sit down and write out what they want. I don't care if you believe you can do it or not. The first goal I set was to have $25,000. I never believed I could have that much. But I found out that if I read it out loud, I'd start to believe it. If you read a lie out loud, you start to believe it. I hit that $25,000 so fast that it made my head spin.

Anyone who wants anything they haven't got should write down what they want in the present tense. It doesn't matter if they think it's silly. They should start reading it and speaking it out loud over and over again. Something will start to happen first in their mind, and then in the outside world—inside out.

Chapter Nine

Making Your Positive Paradigm a Habit for Life

*I*n this final chapter, I want to bring everything that we've been talking about together to show how to make these ideas a habitual way of life.

Ignorance versus Knowledge

There are two paths in life. The first is the path of ignorance. It inevitably leads to worry, doubt, fear, anxiety, depression, and ultimately disease and disintegration.

Ignorance is simply not knowing, but knowledge is omnipresent. There's no need for a person to remain in ignorance. Unfortunately, our educational system is doing very little to teach the subjects we've been talking about. School does not teach you how to take control of your mind. School does not teach you how to respond rather than react. School does not teach you how to stay in a positive frequency or study the laws of the universe. School doesn't teach us anything about paradigms.

Since school never taught us those things, you have to seek them out yourself. There's a lot of information around today on these subjects. Self-help books are on the best-seller list in almost every country today. We've got to start understanding more about ourselves, what's going on around us, and how we either respond or react to it. When ideas come into our mind from other people, we have the ability to accept or reject them. We have the same ability in regard to ideas that we originate ourselves. If we've got a negative idea, it might be right, but that's no reason to dwell on it. There's a negative side to everything. Some people would rather be right than be rich. That's a common saying, and it's true.

We can start from ignorance, doubt, and worry on the conscious level; then, on a subconscious level, the doubt and worry turn into fear. The energy of fear, expressed within and through the body, sets up a vibration known as anxiety. The anxiety is generally suppressed. The suppression turns to depression. The depression turns to disease, and the disease to disintegration.

The polar opposite of ignorance is knowledge. That's the positive path. The knowledge is here and the only way to get to it is to study, but you have to know *what* to study. The libraries are full of knowledge, but knowledge in itself is not power. If it were, all the librarians would be multimillionaires. Most of them have nothing; they're broke. The knowledge has to be organized and intelligently directed. For the past fifty years, with the Proctor Gallagher Institute, I've been organizing and intelligently directing this knowledge.

Understanding and Study

The opposite of doubt and worry, on the positive frequency, is understanding. We want to understand the laws of our being, we want to understand ourselves. We also want to understand there's a power flowing into our consciousness that is without form. We're going to give it form.

The only way to develop understanding is through study. You've got to study the mind and the laws of the universe. When people start studying what we've put together, they'll make great headway. They'll understand that they have to hold an image of what they want. When they internalize it, they develop an emotion called faith, which is the polar opposite of fear.

It's a strange thing: with both faith and fear, you're believing in something you can't see. If you've got a choice, it makes sense to choose faith. Faith is the ability to see the invisible, to believe in the incredible, and that will permit us to receive what the masses call impossible. You see the invisible; you see it in your conscious mind with your imagination. You believe in the incredible. If you take what you see in your imagination and internalize it, turn it over to your subjective mind, which, operating by law, will immediately begin to move it into form. That's believing in the unbelievable.

That has to manifest through the body. We go from the knowledge to understanding to faith. The faith expresses itself in the physical level as well-being, which is the polar opposite of anxiety. Expression turns to acceleration. You're building up speed, because you're at ease. That turns into creation. The polar opposite turns into disintegration.

Your habits can lead you in either of these two directions: toward reinforcing the negative or reinforcing the positive. A habit is an idea that's fixed in the subconscious mind. One paradigm says, don't study. The other part says, study. You set up your habits, and you determine whether you're going to develop good habits.

The Habit of Repetition

When I was young, I was never in the habit of studying. I never studied anything, either in school or when I got out of school. However, after I first heard Earl Nightingale's recordings, I couldn't stop listening to them. Through the repetition of listening to the same thing over and over again, I formed the positive habit of studying. That habit changed my paradigm and changed everything about where I was going and what I was doing. Anyone can do that. If you keep studying this material, good things are going to keep happening.

We're in an age of instant gratification, instant everything, but this process doesn't take place in an instant. It can—all things are possible—but that's rare.

Developing this positive habit of study goes against another part of our paradigm, whereby you read a book, then go on to something different. That's not the way it is here. You get the book, read it, and read it again and again. I have all the original records that Earl Nightingale made, and I listen to them frequently. It's a habit, and that habit has changed my life. I earn millions of dollars today when I used to have difficulty earning thousands. I have work to do all over the world today when I had difficulty finding a job.

The habit of studying the right material will change your paradigm. I've watched people that were castaways in life become useful citizens. When you paradigm changes, your life changes, because the results in life are an expression of the paradigm. The paradigm causes the action, and the action sets up a reaction. As the action and reaction come together, they alter our condition, circumstances, and environment. That's the way it works.

What Do You Really Want?

If we are committed to staying on this pathway of knowledge and to start to produce amazing results in our lives, it's critical to start at the basic level, with the question, what is it that you really want?

The problem with many people is that they don't believe they can have what they want. As little kids we run up to our parents saying, "Mommy, daddy, I want, I want, I want." We want everything under the sun. They'll say, "You can't have everything you want," or "How are you going to get that?" No child can answer that question. When they get older, you can't have everything you want stays as part of the paradigm. When we can grasp that we can have anything we want, we do not have to know how to get it; we only have to know that we *will* get it.

The second you see something in your mind, what you want to realize is where you're going. You've taken your imagination, and you've raised your level of consciousness to a much higher frequency. Now you may only stay there for moments and then go back to where you are. If you get there, stay there for a few minutes; massage that concept, play with it, roll it around in your mind, paint it differently, put yourself in it, see it happening, experience how it will feel. Then say, "I can do it. I don't know how, but I can."

An Oscar, an Emmy, and a Tony

If a person comes to me and says, "This is what I want," I can show them how to get it. There was a movie producer in Los Angeles named Phil Goldfine. Phil was talking to another man, Ed Morrissey, and he asked Ed, "Did you read this book *Born Rich*?"

"Yeah, I know the author."

Phil said, "You don't know him."

"I know him."

"This is an incredible book."

Ed just laughed and said, "OK. I'll phone him," so he phoned me. He said, "Bob, there's a guy here who wants to talk to you."

Phil got on the phone and said, "God, I'd love to sit down to talk to you. Where are you now?"

"I'm in Las Vegas."

"I'm in Los Angeles; could I come and see you?"

"Yeah, if you want."

He came to see me. I sat down and asked, "What do you really want?"

"Millions of dollars."

"What are you earning now?"

"A couple hundred thousand."

"What do you do?"

"I'm a movie producer."

"What else do you want?" He said, "I want to win an Oscar. I want to win an Emmy."

I said, "I can show you how to do all those things, but you've got to do exactly what I tell you."

He said, "I will."

That was around twenty-two or twenty-three years ago. Only twenty-six people have won an Oscar, an Emmy, and a Tony. Phil phoned me in 2019 and said, "I'm going to opening night of *Tootsie*. You want to come to New York?"

"Yes."

I flew down to New York, and I met him. He won his Tony for his musical *Tootsie*. He was the twenty-seventh person to win an Oscar, an Emmy, and a Tony. He's also won gold medals in swimming. He has swum with gold medal Olympians. Whereas the average producer might do two movies in three years, I think Phil is working on twenty-four this year. He'll tell you that he does exactly what I tell him. I said, "I don't care if you believe it or not, I want you to keep telling yourself that this is what happens."

One day Phil sent me a picture of himself holding his Oscar, and he said, "I'm going to win another one."

"That's not the right picture," I said. "Hold the Oscar in one hand, get a picture taken, then hold the Oscar in another hand and get another picture taken. Then have somebody use Photoshop to make it one picture." Hours later, I had a picture back from him with him holding an Oscar in both hands.

Phil earns millions of dollars today. He's told me he's earned up to a million dollars in four hours. He does exactly what I tell him. I don't tell him what time to eat or what time to go to bed, but I've said, "When you sit down and think of what you want, you let your imagination go. If you can see it, write it down. Don't talk to anybody else, but me about it. Because everybody else will laugh at you, and you don't need that happening. Don't mix with people who haven't got big goals. Don't mix with people who want to talk about the news or rough times."

Phil's an excellent example. My partner Sandy Gallagher is another one. You've got to start believing in things that are far out of your reach. If you can see it, it's there. Nothing is created or destroyed. Everything you require is already here. It's a matter of getting in harmony with it. When you're in harmony with it, you'll attract it.

The law of attraction is very clear: the only thing you can attract to you is that which is in harmony with you.

If you're holding an image of poverty, you're never going to attract prosperity.

You've got to see yourself as prosperous. You've got to see yourself with the good you desire. The first thing you have to do is recognize what it is. That's where you sit down and let your mind take off. You put your imagination to work. Phil says the imagination is the most marvelous, miraculous, inconceivably powerful force the world has ever known. He's right. It's the mental tool that takes us to other time zones, to other places, to outer space, to a higher frequency. The imagination will take you anywhere. This isn't something to laugh at; it's something to be in awe of.

Eight Principles for Living

Let me conclude this book by listing the eight principles for living the life you want to live, which I share in my seminars.

1. Develop an awareness of your infinite potential.

That is the beginning of greater good in any aspect of your life. Let there be light. It's sad to see a child who's afraid of the dark. I've always felt that it's much worse to see an adult that's afraid of the light. Let there be light. Let there be a higher degree of conscious awareness. As you become more aware, you'll begin to improve the quality of your life, because it's already here; you just have to become aware of its presence.

2. Act on what you want. Our wants come from the essence of who we are. Our spiritual DNA is perfect; it's in our heart, the heart of hearts, in universal intelligence. You're created in God's image, there's perfection within you, and that perfection is seeking expression within and through you. It is always for expression, expansion, and greater good. Its expression comes to your consciousness as wanting: "I want this." You will go out of your way for what you want. You will do things that are abnormal to get what you want. You'll run when you're weary. You will study when you're tired. Our wants come from the essence of who we are; it's God's or Spirit's way of saying, "Let me work through you to create greater good." Wanting is not getting; getting is a side benefit of wanting. Wanting is growing.

3. Make a decision. Everything you're getting, you're getting because you're programmed to get it. You're in harmony with it. You're not in harmony with what you want; that's why you haven't got it. When you go after what you want, you've got to change the paradigm.

You've often heard the saying, old habits die hard. The paradigm does not want to change; it wants to keep expressing itself over and over again the same way. When you start to go after what you want, the paradigm is going to put up one hell of a fight. You will be very uncomfortable. Everything in you will want to quit. If you don't really understand what you're doing, you will probably quit. If you do understand, the odds are pretty good that you'll keep going. Probably less than 10 percent of people are really going after big goals. Most people don't because they don't really understand that they can have it. A beautiful song sung by Nat King Cole years ago says, "Pretend, pretend you're happy when you're blue." Get the lyrics for that song, read them, study them, memorize them.

4. Total commitment. Commitment separates the professional from the amateur. I believe it was motivational speaker Ken Blanchard who said that when you're interested in something, you'll do it if it's convenient; when you're committed, you'll do it regardless. What you're going after has got to be a committed decision; there is no going back, and there's no quitting. It must happen. Understanding the laws makes it much easier, much more of a pleasant trip.

5. Accountability. Earl Nightingale call this "your success insurance policy." When you have an accountability partner, you're setting up an insurance policy that you're going to keep going. If you're my accountability partner

and I really respect you, I want you to really respect me. If I tell you I'm going to do something and ask you to hold me accountable for it, when the thought of quitting comes to my mind, I'm instantly going to think, what are you going to think of me for doing that? Your accountability partner keeps your nose to the grindstone. This person will get you going when everything wants you to quit. Accountability partners are invaluable. Sandy Gallagher is mine. My son Brian and his associate Peggy McColl are accountability partners. They help each other to an enormous end just because they are accountable to each other. An accountability partner is worth their weight in gold to you. Pick them wisely, and then be accountable to them.

6. Focus. This adds energy and increases the amplitude of vibration. It also directs and increases your personal power. Feeling is conscious awareness of vibration. If you don't feel good, you're in a bad vibration. When you feel good, that indicates you're in a good vibration.

If you're in a shopping mall and somebody behind is staring at you, you will feel it. They're focused on you; they're concentrating on you. They're taking the energy flowing into their consciousness and directing it at you like a laser. Their thoughts hit your brain and set up a vibration. You feel that energy, you feel them staring at you, you turn around, and, sure enough, they are. Concentration increases amplitude of vibration. It takes the energy and speeds up its projection, giving the energy a laserlike focus. That's why focus is so important.

Focus is an act of will. You can develop your will by taking a candle in a holder and putting it opposite your favorite chair. When you're alone, light the candle, sit and stare at the flame, and keep staring at the flame until you become one with the flame. If your mind wanders, which it will, bring it back to the flame. Every time it wanders, bring it back; don't feel bad, just bring it back. You could also put a dot on the wall in front of your favorite chair and stare at that dot. When your mind wanders, bring it back to the dot.

When you can concentrate on one thing, you can concentrate on anything, because you've strengthened your will. The will is the mental faculty that enables you to hold one idea on the screen of the mind. As Emerson said, the only thing that can grow is the thing you give energy to. When you're focused, you're giving more energy to the thing you want.

7. Discipline. I suggest that you commit to reading this book every morning for thirty minutes for sixty days. I also recommend involving a partner in this project. Find a friend. If they don't have a copy of this book, buy one, and give it to them. Write a little note in it. They will love you for it. Then say, "I would like

to study this book with you every day for thirty minutes. Make me accountable, and I'll hold you accountable. At the end of the thirty minutes, we'll check in and discuss what we've learned." If you will commit to doing that, the benefits you've read about in this book will all come to you, because you'll deserve them; you'll have earned them.

8. Visioneering. Visioneering is exercising the imagination to go through the achievement of what you're seeking. It brings order to the mind and attracts to you the things you need in an orderly way. The average person's mind is a helter-skelter of ideas flipping all over the place. When a person is visioneering, they're bringing one thought onto the screen of their mind, and they're focused on it. They're beginning to live it. They've brought order to their mind. Troward said that order is heaven's first law; it's a heavenly thing to visualize. It's a marvelous thing to do. You'll get very good at it. You'll definitely improve your income, your health, your relationships.

Implementing the ideas in this book is a matter of making a firm commitment, picking an accountability partner, and starting right away. Start today, not tomorrow; start right now. Commit the second you read these words. If you're going to give thirty minutes a day, start right now. If you've just spent thirty minutes, spend another thirty. Then tomorrow morning do it again.

Go through this regimen for sixty or ninety days. Earl Nightingale used to say that if you do something for ninety days, you'll probably do it for the rest of your life. I'm inclined to agree with him, because you turn it into a habit.

Study. The rewards you will gain from it are astronomical. They're far beyond what you could ever hope for.